C000281237

7/2

Sea Fishing For Fun

This book is a must for people who enjoy 'messing about in boats' round the coast but who have never enjoyed their boating leisure to the full by trying sea fishing. There's no need to be put off by fears of costly investment in specialised tackle. *Sea Fishing For Fun* scans the immense range of tasty and nourishing food you can catch—and delicious recipes for cooking it.

Widen Your Horizons with this new series

Remember that we cater for all interests. See for yourself with our expanding list of titles.

Places to see

Scottish Islands—Tom Weir
Dartmoor—Crispin Gill

Leisure Activities

Railways for Pleasure—Geoffrey Body
Good Photography Made Easy—Derek Watkins
Looking at Churches—David Bowen

Sporting

The Art of Good Shooting—J. E. M. Ruffer
Archery for All—Daniel Roberts
Rowing for Everyone—Christopher Chant

Holidays

Pony Trekking—Edward Hart

Forthcoming titles

A Guide to Safe Rock Climbing—Patrick Scrivenor
Understanding Castles—Philip Warner

Sea Fishing For Fun

**Alan Wrangles and
Jack P. Tupper**

David & Charles
Newton Abbot   London
North Pomfret (VT)   Vancouver

To James Marcus

ISBN 0 7153 7362 5
Library of Congress Catalog Card Number 76-58794

© Alan Wrangles and Jack P. Tupper 1977

All rights reserved. No part of this
publication may be reproduced, stored
in a retrieval system, or transmitted,
in any form or by any means, electronic,
mechanical, photocopying, recording or
otherwise, without the prior permission
of David & Charles (Publishers) Limited

Set in 12 on 13 Bembo
and printed in Great Britain
by Redwood Burn Limited, Trowbridge and Esher
for David & Charles (Publishers) Limited
Brunel House   Newton Abbot   Devon

Published in the United States of America
by David & Charles Inc
North Pomfret   Vermont 05053   USA

Published in Canada
by Douglas David & Charles Limited
1875 Welch Street   North Vancouver   BC

Contents

Introduction

Although sailing or cruising in a powered craft is certainly an interesting exercise in itself, it can become rather like strolling down a country lane wearing blinkers. Walking for walking's sake is fine, but consider for a moment the amount of beauty and interest missed by the man who just ploughs on ignoring his surroundings.

A large proportion of those who find their sport and relaxation in small craft operate in areas where, for a period of each day, their movements are either severely restricted by low water conditions, or they may be completely aground for a spell. This period can frequently be used to great advantage. Instead of regretting the lack of water and loss of sailing time, why not make the most of this short period not only to study the beauty of what has been uncovered by the receding tide, but also to exploit the sea in a manner you may not have even considered?

It is in fact quite possible to extract a vast quantity of varied and tasty foods from the sea and its bed, without great amounts of specialised knowledge and expensive equipment. But it must be realised from the start that becoming in any way involved with catching fish can have drastic results. It frequently happens that a person who begins fishing for fun ends up by taking the sport extremely seriously and developing great ambitions to catch the uncatchable, so be warned!

1 Where can I Fish, and What For?

There is an enormous variety of sea food just waiting to be dug up, picked up or caught: it is just a matter of knowing where, when and how to look, how to arrange a few basic items of tackle, and what to do with the creatures once you have got them.

'All very simple,' you may say, 'but surely there are some rules and regulations to obey?'

There is a clear distinction between the *open sea*, that area beyond the 3–mile limit, and the *close inshore waters*, the saltings, mud flats and the bed of any estuary, creek, inlet or natural harbour. It is accepted that the general public have the right to take fish in tidal waters. However, where there is what is known as a 'several fishery', this right to fish freely does not exist. In this context the word 'several' means 'separate', 'distinct' or 'individual', and a 'several' fishery is one where the right to fish is enjoyed by a 'separate' or 'distinct' person, who may of course grant another person or persons the right to fish in that particular area.

It is interesting to note that some of the 'several fisheries' which exist today are a link with the past, as, with the signing of Magna Carta, the right of the Crown to create such fisheries in tidal waters was abolished. Today, only Parliament can deprive us of our age-old right to fish in public waters.

All this may seem exceedingly complicated and unnecessary when looked at in relation to collecting a few mussels or winkles. In fact the average boat owner need not worry himself overmuch regarding these rights, except where notices proclaim the existence of such rights, and where creatures such as oysters and game fish are concerned.

The limits of a several fishery are usually well marked, not only to warn would-be poachers, but also as an indication to those, the vast majority, who will always respect another man's property. The point here is that walking across or bait-digging in an area seeded with oysters or clams could do as much damage as walking through a field of standing corn. Both corn and clams are crops, both are being tended, and both could represent a large capital investment.

But areas where the sea bed is 'farmed' in this way are relatively few and far between, and the greater part of the sea bed is freely available to anyone. However, there are a few rules and regulations which are designed to protect the young of certain species of fish, some crustaceans—and the public.

How do you know whether or not the shellfish in a particular area are contaminated, or even if local byelaws prohibit the collection of certain shellfish at particular times of the year? Quite easily: contact the local Chief Fishery Officer. He can be traced either through the local telephone directory, harbourmaster or coastguard. These officers are always most helpful, and are also a mine of very useful information.

When cruising or taking a holiday away from familiar ground it might well pay dividends to write to the local Chief Fishery Officer and ask for a copy of the district byelaws. These frequently differ from area to area, and they can have a direct bearing on what one may or may not do when reaping the harvest of the sea, and not purely sport fishing with a rod and line.

Although these two pastimes may go hand in hand in some ways, there is a dividing line, and it is as well to understand just where it is drawn.

The Ministry of Agriculture, Fisheries and Food appoints District Inspectors whose areas may cover 200 miles or more of coastline; and in a general sense they are concerned with what happens in offshore waters, beyond the 3-mile limit.

Working at a local level, but still in contact with the Ministry District Inspectors, there are Chief Fishery Officers (CFOs) and their assistants. The CFOs are employed by committees which lay down rules and regulations which are designed to suit the area which they control, and this may be a whole county, or possibly two.

With the rapid increase in the numbers of those who fish using methods other than a rod and line, it is vital to understand and obey the various local byelaws and other regulations which, from time to time may apply.

Protected Fish

The *Sea-Fishing Industry (Immature Sea Fish) Order* (1968) sets out quite clearly the species which are protected, and the size below which it is an offence to land them. Obviously no one is able to avoid catching small or immature fish, and there is certainly no offence in so doing, but—and this is most important—an immature fish of a protected species should be released and returned to the sea alive as soon as possible.

The species which are protected by law, and the size below which they should not be kept are as follows:

	Cm	In
cod	30	11.8
haddock	27	10.6
hake	30	11.8
plaice	25	9.8
witch	28	11.0
lemon sole	25	9.8
sole	24	9.4
turbot	30	11.8
brill	30	11.8
megrim	25	9.8
whiting	25	9.8
dab	15	5.9
bass	26	10.4

Although correct at the time of writing, alterations and additions to the list can be made at any time. Remember that you, the fisherman, are required to know the law.

The *Sea Fishing Industry (Crabs and Lobsters) Order* of 1976 lays down minimum sizes below which these animals must not be landed. At the time of writing a crab must not be less than 4½in (114mm) across the broadest part of its back, or a lobster less than 3in (80mm) from the end of the carapace to an eye socket. (*Note*: although correct at the time of writing, new regulations regarding crab measurements are expected.)

If you own a small craft and decide to invest in a small trawl, or one or two trammel nets, you must make certain that the nets you use comply with the local byelaws. Not only must the net sizes be right, but the user must also be absolutely certain that he is using the right net at the right place at the appropriate time, and that catches comply with catch limits.

Apart from the measure of protection to certain species which springs from the *Sea Fishing Industry Order* of 1968, there are other rules regarding size limits which have been laid down by various sportfishing bodies such as the Welsh, Northern, National, Cornish and Scottish Federations. These are the parent bodies to which vast numbers of city, town, village and works based clubs look to for help, guidance, and support when their various interests are being threatened.

It is, I feel, well worth noting some of the size limits which their members are expected to recognise. For example, the National Federation of Sea Anglers ask all who belong to affiliated clubs not to keep black bream measuring less than 9in or bass less than 15in from tail fork to nose. Similar restrictions apply to species such as conger eel, dabs and garfish which have NFSA size limits of 28in, 8in and 15in, respectively.

In answer to the obvious question 'why do angling associations set size limits on species which are not covered by law?' I would say quite simply, in an effort to conserve fish stocks and to introduce certain standards into an ever-expanding sport.

It is also true that individual fish of a size below that set by the various amateur associations are hardly worth considering for the pot or pan. For example, when both head and tail are removed from a flounder less than 9in from nose to tail fork, there is very little left to eat.

At the time of writing, the following are the size limits set by the NFSA, and it will be noted that skate and ray have a weight, not length limit:

Size Limit Table

	In
bass	15
bream, black	9
bream, red	9
brill	14
bull huss	23
cod	12
conger	28
dab	8
eel, silver	12
flounder	9
garfish	15
gurnard	9
mullet, grey	13
mullet, red	13
mackerel	11
plaice	10
pollack	12
pouting	10
sole	$9\frac{1}{2}$
turbot	16
weaver	8
whiting	10
wrasse	9

1 Uncommon flatfish—the megrim. An interesting, almost dab-shaped, fish which makes excellent eating

	Lb
skate, common	5
thornback	5

(*Note*: In some areas larger limits apply for flounder.)

The above list is not complete. Various species of shark have not been included and of course from time to time modifications can be and are made to such lists.

Learning to recognise what is good to eat, although unattractive when freshly caught, is all part of the game, and there is a certain amount of satisfaction in being able to say to children, as they pull a squirming fish over the side, 'That's for supper, it's a dogfish, good to eat once it's skinned, but watch out, its skin is very rough and may graze your hand or arm'.

And therein lies the secret of fishing for fun: recognising what you have caught, and knowing what to do with it.

2 Lobsters, Crabs, Prawns and Shrimps

Common lobster

The lobster is a voracious carnivore, and its food consists mainly of fish, anemones and limpets. It is always considered that lobsters prefer fish bait which has not been allowed to become 'high', but the use of stale bait is common practice as it discourages crabs, who prefer fresh bait, from occupying the pots or traps.

Generally, the male lobster has larger claws and a narrow body, whereas the female has a relatively larger and broader tail to accommodate the eggs or 'berries' which are attached in clusters to the swimmerets.

Lobsters are common all round the British Isles, but only in areas where there are weed-covered rocks or broken ground which provides adequate shelter at all times. They tend to live in deeper water away from the shore during the winter, but come inshore to spread throughout relatively shallow water, and even into areas abutting the low water mark, during the summer and early autumn. In some areas, the period when lobsters become most plentiful is known to the local fishermen as the 'crawl'.

If you are thinking of catching lobsters, it is wise to check on the local byelaws. There may be regulations governing both the size and the taking of 'berried' lobsters.

Spiny lobster

Along the south and south-west coasts of England, there is also the spiny lobster or sea crawfish. Its name is derived from the fact that its body is covered with spines. It also has exceptionally long antennae, a total absence of pincer claws on any of its five pairs of legs, and no main claws, as has the common lobster.

Norwegian lobster

The Norwegian lobster, commonly known as the 'Dublin Bay prawn', is generally only caught by professional fishermen operating in deep water, and is often retailed under the name of 'scampi', although this name really refers to the dish, rather than to the fish itself.

Common prawn

Very little is known about the life history of the common prawn. It inhabits deep water, living in shoals. Prawns are creatures with a well developed shoal instinct. They also seem to prefer rocky or broken ground.

Prawns tend to come fairly close inshore during the period from March until November. They are affected by a variety of conditions and seem to be able to foretell bad weather well in advance. This enables them to retire into deeper water, and therefore escape the ensuing buffeting and the danger of being thrown up onto the foreshore by heavy seas.

On occasions small prawns are sold as shrimps. This is not to say that deception is being practised; it is just a result of the animals being caught together, and being of a similar size they are marketed as one. Small prawns are pale pink or orangey-red in colour and they can be distinguished from shrimps as the latter do not have a sharp jagged spike on the carapace or rostrum; they are brown when cooked.

Shrimp

Shrimps when caught are a pale, transparent, grey colour, assuming a brownish hue when cooked. They are also, generally, substantially smaller than prawns and can only be caught in areas where there is soft sand, some weed and sandy pools.

Although, generally speaking, prawns are most common in the south and west of the country, there are other areas where they can be caught and local enquiries will usually reveal whatever possibilities may exist. Shrimps, however, tend to be more widely distributed, but inshore pollution has taken, and is still taking, a toll, and areas where at one time these animals were prolific are now barren.

Edible crab

The edible crab is found occupying similar areas to the lobster. However, it is much slower in all its movements and incapable of swimming. It relies on its legs to gain access to any area or part of a rock. The male crab has a larger pincer than the female and also has a formidable grip.

The edible crab's food is similar to that of the lobster, but it has a preference for fresh bait or fresh fish. Like the lobster, the crab does not assume its pink to red colour until it has been cooked. When fresh from the sea the shell has a translucent orange to pale-brown colour.

During the summer months when very low spring tides occur, crabs can be found marooned above the low water mark, while lobsters generally manage to keep within sufficient water to protect themselves.

Pots, traps, and nets

Professional fishermen take lobsters and crabs in specially manufactured pots or traps. These may be constructed of willow and shaped rather like an old fashioned beehive, or they may have a wood and iron framework covered by netting. Both types are weighted at the bottom to keep them anchored to the sea bed.

It is always possible to obtain old lobster pots which can be made quite serviceable after some repairs have been effected. However, always remember that although the sea is free it would be most unfair to set the pots where the local fishermen are already engaged in earning a living. With this thought in mind, approach the local fishermen and ask where one or two of your own pots could be set without interfering with theirs. Often there are small areas of rock or broken ground which are too restricted for them to bother with.

Pots are baited with fish, 'high' or stale bait being used for lobsters, and fresh bait for crabs. The crustaceans enter the pots through a funnel which is formed for this purpose, and once in the main part of the pot where they can reach the bait, they become trapped. The bait must be fixed in position where it cannot be reached by lobsters and crabs outside the pot, nor should it be possible for them to reach the bait without actually entering the pot completely.

If your boat is too small to carry pots, it may be worth considering hunting along the shoreline for lobsters and crabs during periods of low water, especially when spring tides are running. Bear in mind that generally speaking lobsters are nocturnal beasts; they feed mainly at night and therefore the best chances of catching them are during the latter part of the evening or early morning, particularly between first light and sunrise.

Catching lobsters

Lobsters can be caught in a variety of ways, some of which require a considerable amount of skill, but one of the simplest methods is using a baited drop net, one similar to that used for catching prawns. A drop net consists of a large galvanised ring supported by three drop cords which join at a point approximately 18in above the net, and in turn are supported in the water by a small piece of cork. The main lifting line rising to the surface is also provided with adequate floats.

The net itself forms a bag underneath the frame, and the bait is supported by a wire or string which is stretched tightly across the mouth of the net.

Lower the net so that the lobster can enter easily without fouling the supporting strings with its claws. Once the lobster is over the net and feeding, the net can be gently raised and the victim trapped in the bottom. Once the first movement has been made, the net must be raised with all speed.

On many occasions a careful inspection of the rocky area

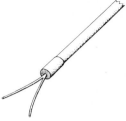

Fig 1 Simple lobster pole

one is fishing will reveal a lobster lying at the entrance to its hole, its claws apparently folded across its body. Do not be fooled by what may appear to be a 'carefree' attitude on the part of the lobster. They are wary creatures, and be assured it will have spotted you. Its whole existence is geared to careful watchfulness.

In spite of the lobster's distinctive colour it is not easily seen, and more likely than not you will first spot its red feelers or the white inner edges of its claws.

Once a lobster is found, be careful not to disturb it. Lure it out from its hole by lowering some bait, attached to a suitable weight, to a point 2 or 3ft in front of its lair. Both patience and care are essential, as any undue movement or splashing will undoubtedly cause the lobster to seek safety before you are ready.

As soon as the bait has lured the animal out from its hole, a prawn or lobster net can be slipped into position to cover its retreat. As soon as all is ready, the creature can be disturbed, and it will immediately back into the prepared trap. At this point you must raise the net as quickly as possible so that it cannot turn round and back out of the net with as much speed as it went into it.

Lobster poles and hooks

When it proves impossible to lure a lobster from its hole—or it refuses to move out more than an inch or so—another tactic can be employed. A long rod or handle is needed, for example an ordinary broom handle, fitted with a brass or copper ferrule to stop the end splitting when two light steel, or galvanised iron, wires are inserted and then sprung to form a V—shape.

A lobster pole is used in much the same manner as a countryman would use a vermin stick: to reach gingerly down and pin the lobster across its 'shoulders'.

Another alternative is to use a lobster hook. This is an easily constructed gadget which can be made from a length of hazel wood with a large fish hook fixed to the end. Certain modifications need to be carried out to the hook. For example, the point should not run absolutely parallel with the shaft; it needs to be slightly turned outwards, and can be slightly blunted (this should not be overdone; the hook still needs to be comparatively sharp).

The lobster hook can be used to search all likely holes and under rocks, and if a lobster is found—here again only experience will give the 'feel' for an operation of this sort—it can be hooked out.

Frequently in large expanses of rock the lobster hunter may find quite sizeable and irregularly shaped pools, and assuming that other environmental factors are suitable it is more than reasonable to expect one or more lobsters to be in residence. However, trying to catch a lobster under these conditions is rather like playing blind man's buff, with the hunter being even more restricted than usual by attempting to operate in an alien element.

There are several things that can be done to give you at least an even chance. Bear in mind that lobsters will always head for the deepest possible water, and so if one side of the hole is shallower than the other it is reasonable to assume that the lobster will be in the deeper section. Use both hook and net, the net being held in readiness to prevent the creature's escape.

On certain stretches of coastline the action of the sea on the cliffs has resulted in a vast array of slab-like stones littering the sea bed, sections of which will be uncovered on long spring tides. It is well worth while turning over such slabs and checking whether or not lobsters or other interesting crustaceans may be hiding beneath them.

It could well be that a protruding feeler or claw may give away the exact location of the animal you are hunting, and this fact will enable you to make your plans before you lift what could well be an extremely heavy piece of stone. Try to work out where the lobster will go if and when you move the stone.

You may need to cut off its means of escape by positioning a prawn or lobster net, or it may be possible to hook the animal out very quickly and neatly with a lobster hook. To be successful you must think ahead but the real key to successful hunting of this kind is pure experience.

There is one very important fact to remember, and unfortunately on so many occasions the amateur fisherman tends to ignore this vital detail. Carefully replace every rock you lift. Once these places are disturbed and the chain of life broken down, the larger animals such as lobsters and crabs will not reinhabit the disturbed areas.

Catching crabs

The edible crab is also a familiar sight, although most people have often only seen it lying on a fishmonger's slab, where its reddish-coloured shell and black-tipped claws make it extremely distinctive.

Crabs are normally taken in traps set in fairly deep water, and catching crabs along the shoreline must be considered as a sideline to prawning or lobstering. It must also be realised that when crabs are found sheltering, they may be hiding because they are changing their shells. The flesh of a soft-shelled crab is sometimes bitter and unpalatable.

Crabs are frequently quite content to be left by the receding tide so long as the chosen lair is well camouflaged by overhanging weed, and they favour places in which an amount of water has been left. The edible crabs found along the shore are seldom very large, generally only 4–5in across, a size which can be easily handled. But be careful! A large crab in a confined space may press its body upwards, trapping your hand between its back and the ceiling of its cavern; its pincer may also seize part of your hand or a finger in a vice-like grip, and you could suffer quite considerably, especially if the tide is rising around you.

Prawning

Prawning is an altogether different method of fishing. It can be carried out in conjunction with hunting lobsters and crabs, but the tendency is to concentrate on one or the other, particularly as prawns are far more widespread and lobster holes generally few and far between.

Making a prawning net

Prawns are normally caught in either of two generally accepted methods—push net or baited drop net. Regarding the former, it is extremely difficult to buy suitable ones; often those on sale are poorly made and structurally weak, and the net incorrectly shaped.

The best type of hand net is equipped with a stout ash handle to which is fitted a copper or brass ferrule to prevent the end (where a galvanised iron ring is fitted) from splitting. The ring should be formed into an oval shape, slightly pointed at the front. The main part of the net frame should consist of a flat strip of galvanised iron about $\frac{5}{8}$in wide and $\frac{1}{8}$-$\frac{3}{16}$in thick. Ideally it should be about 13in across the broadest part and about 16in long. The netting is suspended from a copper or galvanised iron wire threaded through brass or copper rivets which in turn are set in holes in the main part of the frame. When a net is made like this, the outer edge of the galvanised iron takes all the abrasion and shock associated with prawning among rock and shingle.

As an alternative, take a $\frac{3}{8}$in mild steel rod, bend it into an oval of approximately similar size and weld it at one end so that a spike is formed, which, in turn, can be driven into a ferruled handle. The net is then mounted on a relatively thick piece of galvanised iron wire, and this is wired to the inside of the main metal frame. Once again use galvanised iron wire and twist the ends of each loop down out of the way.

By using either of these methods you will have a net which is protected, a most important fact when considering the use to which it is put.

The net itself needs to be correctly shaped; frequently they are either too shallow or too voluminous. If it is too shallow the catch can leap clear, or there could possibly be insufficient depth to hold a lobster. On the other hand, if the net is too deep then the prawns will be spread all over the bottom and sides when trapped, and the time taken to pick them out is time lost for fishing. And time is of the essence. During the low water period of spring tides you are given the chance to explore a great many marks which are normally covered; but spring tides move very quickly. The area is only uncovered for a relatively short space of time, sometimes for only 15 or 30 minutes at the most before the incoming tide makes fishing impossible.

For efficiency's sake you need a net of around 12in in depth. Try not to give it a pointed end; if you do, all the prawns, weed, rubbish and any other debris settle right into the bottom of the net and become almost impossible to sort out in the time available to you.

The best nets for this kind of work are made from sleeve netting, the type which is available in tackle shops and is frequently used by freshwater anglers to make keep nets. Fix the net to the main ring, let it hang in a cylinder, then cut triangular sections from the bottom edge; sew the edges together and gather them at the base. An extremely good net shape can be made in this way. Do not make the whole net too heavy: some of the holes into which it may be thrust could be so deep that the whole weight of the net, frame and pole could be placed on the wrist, while the net must still be operated.

It is vital for the metal frame holding the net to be securely set into the wooden handle. If this is not done you may well find that the net ring is left in an irretrievable position under rocks. It is also a good idea to paint the end of the net handle with a very distinctive colour so that it can be easily spotted if left lying on the foreshore.

Using a push or dip net

Prawning with a push or dip net is comparatively easy once you know where the prawns are to be caught. Small shallow recesses under the base of rocks which in turn are overhung with weed are ideal places. And it is always possible that both prawns and lobsters will be found in the same pool. Try pushing the net into the hole and down one side, keeping it almost flat; the prawns will retreat from the face of the net which can then be turned by a twisting action so that it is half open, then bring it back along the other side of the hole. In so doing the prawns should be trapped.

2 Rock pool at low tide—a good hunting-ground not only for prawns but often for peeler and softback crabs

Fig 2 Two-ring drop net

As you bring the net up to the entrance of the hole, try to use your free hand to frighten back any prawns which may be swimming ahead of the net. Do not forget to search every nook and cranny, and remember that in very shallow water prawns may even jump clear of the water in their efforts to escape the net.

Never be depressed if you have trouble finding prawns in an area where the locals are obviously enjoying a fair amount of success; they will naturally know the area better than you. Successful prawning demands persistence, patience and a willingness to get wet, sometimes up to your armpits. It is no good expecting to find prawns in every pool, but where you find a likely place it must be searched thoroughly to get the best results.

Prawns will often gather at the entrance of a suitable shelter hole in the rocks and appear to 'sun' themselves against a rock face. As you approach they will sink out of sight, possibly leaving only their feelers visible. They can also hang upside down, suspended from the 'ceiling', while clinging to weed or the rough surface of rock—hence the need for a thorough search of every part of the pool and all the rocky surround.

Using a drop net

The baited drop net method of catching prawns is certainly more leisurely; it demands far less exertion; but it is in many ways less fun. The net is formed either with a single ring, one having a comparatively shallow net slung underneath, or

23

with a double ring.

The single ring and shallow net has the bait threaded onto wire or cord which runs straight across the net opening from one side of the ring to the other. The double-ring prawn net is similar, but has a slightly smaller base ring connected to the main ring by a cylinder of netting. There is also a semi-rigid flat base of netting which is weighted to carry the net to the bottom.

These nets can be made from either nylon or Terylene and the base of the two-ring net is formed with a type of plastic netting, for example Netlon. Always use small mesh; approximately $\frac{1}{4}$in square net is ideal.

There are certain advantages in using this type of net— mainly that it is rotproof. It is also more efficient—as soon as lifting begins, a curtain rises on either side of the feeding prawns and this helps to trap them even more effectively.

Prawns are not particular whether the bait is fresh or stale. By nature they are scavengers, and various baits can be used, such as leftovers from plaice and other flatfish fillets. The backbone and head of a fish skeleton will spread over quite a wide area at the bottom of a double ring net, and it can be fixed to the base where it will attract prawns in quite large numbers. Alternatively, use stale fish or even pieces of kipper—not only extremely suitable, but always available.

Never be mean with bait when fishing for prawns; there is a tendency for just one prawn to feed if only one small piece of bait is fixed in the centre of the net, and in this situation others will not venture in to disturb the animal which is already in possession of the food supply. But if the bait is well spread across the bottom of the net, and if the net is large enough, six or more prawns could well be enticed in to feed. With other prawns hovering around, it could be a very profitable exercise.

You can use more than one net, but be sensible; there are various problems associated with trying to use too many nets, and not least is the menace created by the small greenback or shore crab. These can smother a net very quickly and will gorge themselves, leaving you with an empty net. The greenback crabs you catch should not be put back into the water close to the drop net, as every broken or crushed greenback forms an alternative feeding area for the prawns. Any crabs that have been crushed or broken should be left high on the rocks; they will be swept off by the tide and eaten by other predators.

When working from a boat do not drop your nets at random. Search out the likely areas, work your nets systematically, and do not waste your time in unproductive areas. If you stick to the more shallow areas and use a pair of polaroid glasses, you should be able to spot many likely places.

When hunting lobsters, crabs, prawns and shrimps, and indeed any of the edible creatures provided by the sea, thought must be given to the containers you will use while working. Virtually any bag or sack will hold a lobster or crab, but it is wise to wrap each individual lobster in sacking before placing it in the bag. Alternatively, tie the claws to prevent them tearing each other to pieces while in captivity. The ferocity lobsters display is frightening: place two lobsters (or crabs) together and within minutes they will begin a fight to the death. Keep the sacking clean and well soaked in sea water; there is nothing worse than storing lobsters and crabs in dank, evil-smelling bags.

Prawns are easily crushed, and although they can be cooked and eaten even in this condition, they present a rather poor appearance. An ideal prawning bag is one of the old wartime canvas gas-mask cases. These are rectangular, approximately 15in deep and about 9in wide. Cut the dividing partitions and remove them, then fit a piece of stiff wire around the entrance so that the mouth of the bag can be kept open while you are working. The bottom of the bag, being fitted with brass ventilators, will allow any surplus water to drain. You can therefore keep the prawns fresh by pouring a drop of water over them every so often.

Watch out for your own carelessness. The bag can be crushed if you either slip or sit on it, and, of course, if you up-end the bag all your good work will be lost.

Prawns, as mentioned earlier, are greatly affected by weather changes. In fact they may well vacate the foreshore well in advance of bad weather, and so if you are fishing in an area where it is known prawns are to be caught, do not be discouraged by a sudden lack of these creatures. Rather, be wise and heed their warning.

In this chapter there has been a tendancy to place crabs, lobsters and prawns in similar locations. Do not take this literally and apply rigidly to any or every section of coast. Prawns may be caught at one point, prawns and crabs at another, but only lobsters at a third. Obviously there are very few places where all three will be found together, and do not be misled into believing that a lobster is hiding under every stone on a well used beach. Nothing could be further from the truth.

Shrimping

Finally, a few words about shrimping. Generally speaking shrimps are only found on sandy foreshores where pollution is not severe enough to drive them away. They are collected by using a strand net similar in general design and pattern to the shrimping net sold by shops in seaside resorts. The main difference is that the net should be much larger, with a stouter handle and supporting members to the main frontboard.

The net is pushed down hard onto the sand and run along with the tide for a distance of 50–60yd, when it should be raised and the catch cleared. A bag such as the one previously mentioned for prawns can be used to hold the catch.

Finally, a word of warning. Learn to identify that most dangerous fish, the weever. They are frequently scooped up when shrimping; do not dive your hands into a catch, tip it out and be careful as you sort the shrimps from the weed.

A sting from a weever fish needs medical attention.

3 Choosing Your Tackle

As this book is about sea fishing in its broadest sense, as distinct from pure angling, this chapter is not a catalogue of equipment normally associated with sport fishing or angling. However, it is a very short step from laying a simple trotline to using a handline; and once the handline stage is reached the allure of rod and reel is hard to resist. Therefore an ideal starting-place is the point of contact between man and fish—the hook.

Hooks—a simple guide

The first essential is an extremely sharp point, giving good penetration. If the fish can be held on the bottom of the hook's bend, the hook will be able to give of its best because this is its strongest part. Some fish are extremely strong, and if the hook fails to penetrate properly it is quite possible for some of the stronger species to straighten it out to such an extent that they break free.

The type of bait to be used has a great bearing on the type of hook. For example, fishing for plaice and baiting with worm calls for a hook made from thin wire, and preferably a long shank with an eyed end for easy fixing. But a long-shank, thin-wire hook would not be suitable for ray or other species where large baits are employed. Forged steel hooks (such as Seamaster) are ideal when using a bait such as a slice of mackerel.

The novice need only remember that a vast assortment of hooks in a wide range of sizes is available, and know how and why to select a limited number which will suit most requirements.

When it comes to hook size, hooks numbered 2, 4, 6, 8 and so on, get smaller as the number gets higher, and in a general sense these smaller hooks are designed for freshwater fishing. Hooks generally accepted as being suitable for sea fishing start at size 1 and get larger as they progress through 1/0, 2/0, 3/0 and on until sizes 12/0 and 14/0 are reached—but hooks of this size are designed for shark and other species which have huge mouths and are attracted by large baits such as whole fish of possibly 2lb or more. These 'big game' fish are beyond the scope of this book.

Correct hook selection is vital. Large hooks with small baits are, in their own way, just as inefficient as small hooks covered with excess bait.

Lines

Lines fall into two distinct categories; those which stretch and those which do not. The line most widely used is *nylon monofilament:* a single strand of nylon possessing a degree of elasticity. It is also relatively cheap, readily available, and the most efficient line to use with a fixed-spool reel (see p30).

The other type of line is normally braided, and may be sold under any one of a number of different trade names. The material used is always a man-made fibre as this is rotproof and usually has a far greater life span than the old style natural fibres.

There are other types of line, for example stainless-steel wire line and metal-cored line, but these are really beyond the scope of those who wish merely to fish for fun. These are specialist lines and are extremely expensive compared with nylon monofilament, which is favoured by the vast majority of anglers.

Most nylon lines are sold as having a particular breaking strain or BS. In other words a line said to have a 10lb BS can be relied upon, while it is in good condition, to absorb a steady strain of 10lb, although the snatch or strain suddenly imposed by a 10lb weight being dropped would almost certainly break it.

The amount of additional strain that a 10lb BS line will

take is problematical. Some may absorb another 2 or 3lb, or even 4lb, whereas some 10lb BS lines may snap at 11lb. This does not mean that the lines which snap at 11lb are inferior to those '10lb BS lines' which snap at 14lb. Some manufacturers sell a line with a higher breaking strain under a lower rating.

The other method used to denote the strength of the line is by giving it a test rating. In other words this line is manufactured under controlled conditions and is guaranteed to break just before a given strain is placed upon it. If the line were a 10lb test line, it could be relied upon to snap when the strain reached about 9lb or maybe just slightly more, but it would not stand up to the full 10lb.

The reason why test-class lines exist can be found by examining the rules and regulations of the International Game Fishing Association. All world records recognised by the IGFA fall into test classes. Lines used for this style of fishing are advertised as 'conforming to IGFA standards'.

The inbuilt springiness or elasticity contained by nylon monofilament is both useful and tricky. It is useful because it helps to absorb the thrust and strain imposed upon it by the leaping and lunging of a heavy fish; but when well stretched nylon line is wound onto a spool it exerts great crushing pressure, the sort of pressure which can completely distort a reel not built for the task you are asking it to perform.

Frequently the amateur fisherman uses line which is far too heavy or strong for the rod and reel. There is very little point in using 80lb breaking strain line on a rod which will snap long before that amount of strain is reached. In a general sense the average type of boat rod used by the occasional fisherman is well served with a 30lb BS line, but more advice on the relationship between rod and line is given in the section dealing with rods.

In simple terms nylon monofilament line can be used on either a revolving-drum reel or a fixed-spool reel, but it is a must if you use a fixed-spool reel for the reasons given in the section dealing with reels.

Frequently, anglers fishing in deep water prefer to use braided line because its lack of elasticity enables them to acquire a greater sense of 'touch'. In other words they feel more directly in contact with the lead, and they are able to tell when the weight touches the bottom. They can also strike at a biting fish more rapidly. The elasticity in nylon monofilament can mask the sensation of both touch and a bite.

There are various other types of line which are of little importance to the occasional fisherman, but information regarding nylon-covered, twisted-steel line such as Steelon is useful. This material is used to form traces when fishing for species such as tope, ray and conger, as these fish have either extremely sharp teeth and powerful jaws, or their skin is such that it can rasp through the softer monofilament or braided line. Further details regarding this material are given on page 36.

Reels

Basically there are four types of reel, the simplest being the *centre-pin*—a reel in which the drum or spool revolves once for every turn of the handle. This is known as a direct-drive reel.

The *multiplying reel* has a drum which revolves more rapidly than the handle is turned, the drive being passed through a system of gears. Normally there is also a 'drag'. This is a friction plate, placed between the crank handle and drive gear, which can be adjusted so that the greater the pressure placed upon the plate, the harder it is for the spool to turn and give line automatically.

A *fixed-spool* reel is, as its name implies, a reel which does not depend upon a revolving spool to give line. This piece of equipment is widely used and also widely abused, but for all that they sell in vast quantities and seem to put up with a tremendous amount of punishment.

A fixed-spool reel uses a *bale arm* or *flyer* to spread the line on the spool. There is a cunningly designed drive mechanism which, as the crank handle is turned, not only turns the bale arm around the fixed spool, but also moves the spool backwards and forwards, ensuring that the line is laid evenly onto the spool. The spool does not revolve when delivering line, except when under strain.

To cast with a fixed-spool reel, the rod is held in one hand and the line is picked up on the ball of the index or forefinger of the hand holding the rod. The bale arm is opened downwards with the other hand. Never trap the line between your forefinger and rod: the line should just rest across the ball of the forefinger, being held under tension by the weight of the lead and bait.

When you are ready to cast, swing the rod tip slowly behind your body, and focus your eyes on an imaginary point some 2ft or so above the target you wish to hit. Flick the rod tip forward and, as the bait swings around towards the target, release your forefinger and the bait will fly through the air.

3 In such circumstances the angler must beware the reel. The speed at which the drum would revolve if his hand slipped could easily break a finger

No matter whether you are using a fixed-spool, a multi-plying or a side-cast reel, do not try to be too enthusiastic at first. Get the feel of the equipment and only try to achieve relatively short distances. For example, 15 or 20yd is as much as you should try when beginning with a fixed-spool reel. However, within an hour or so, casts of 30–50yd can be achieved with quite commendable accuracy.

Various arrangements of hand, rod, finger and line will be seen in use, but all of them are not only considerably more difficult than the method just described, they are also far less efficient.

It is also important to set the tension nut on a fixed-spool reel in the correct position. These reels are designed to react when excessive strain is placed upon the line and rod. The spool will revolve against a friction plate and give line auto-matically, minimising the risk of either line or rod failure.

Before casting hold the end of the line and pull until the rod tip comes round to a point roughly 45 degrees to the butt. At this point the spool should begin to give line. If it does not, slacken the tension nut until the spool begins to turn slowly. If the spool slips before the rod tip reaches the 45 degree angle, just tighten the tension nut slightly until the correct balance is achieved.

If, while you are playing a fish, the bale arm fails to recover line as you turn the handle, do not under any circumstances keep winding. If you do, this will only add so much twist to your monofilament line that it will kink and snarl up im-mediately the tension is released.

The fixed-spool reel was never designed to lift heavy weights. To use a small reel designed for freshwater use is to ask for trouble in sea fishing, where leads of 4, 6 or 8oz are relatively commonplace. This type of reel was developed with the express purpose of allowing the angler to achieve long and accurate casts with relatively light weights, and, with the gear ratio of about 3:1, to recover line extremely rapidly.

4 Beach anglers in action from a promenade at high tide. Their long rods need a specialised technique to punch the tackle far out beyond the surf. However, when fishing from such a position, remember passers-by

In recent years fixed-spool reels have become widely used, and greatly strengthened models are now much favoured by sea anglers. Despite these improvements, it does not alter the basic fact that fixed-spool reels and heavy weights are not really compatible. Therefore, as you would not expect a car to climb a steep hill slowly in fourth gear, do not expect your reel to perform tasks for which it was not designed.

The *multiplying reel* is basically a sophisticated version of the simple, direct-drive, centre-pin reel. It is always placed on top of the rod so that the spool can be controlled by the angler's thumb.

The reel consists of a metal or plastic spool, a spool housing and a series of gears connected to the crank handle through a friction or clutch plate. The controls on a multiplying reel may vary slightly from model to model, but they normally consist of a button on the end plate opposite the handle, which engages or disengages a ratchet device, to stop the spool from turning freely and give audible warning if a fish draws line. Another lever or button disengages the gears from the spool; the gears may or may not engage auto-matically when the crank-handle is turned. Finally there is a star-shaped wheel on the crank-handle spindle, just behind the handle, which controls the amount of tension on the clutch.

Usually, reels with metal spools are used by boat fishermen, and those equipped with plastic spools are for beach anglers who often need to cast long distances. A metal spool is necessary for boat angling because the heavier weights and greater depths fished by boat anglers mean that the nylon line being used is placed under more stress, and therefore will exert a far greater crushing force on the spool when reeled in.

There are other reasons why metal or heavily reinforced plastic spools are used by boat fishermen and not by beach anglers. These include the fact that additional energy is necessary to set a heavy spool turning, thus restricting to some extent the distance which can be cast; there is also the flywheel effect of a revolving metal spool. Both these features affect the efficiency of beach-casting techniques.

Remembering that the angler's thumb is frequently used to control the rapidly spinning spool, it can be understood why beach anglers are rather loath to use a multiplying reel with a heavy metal spool. This would obviously be far more difficult to stop, and could result in a vast number of burned thumbs.

The star drag or clutch-tensioning control is used and set in such a way that the spool will automatically revolve and give line when excessive strain is placed upon it. This feature is in effect a 'safety valve', and if correctly set should obviate the risk of either line or rod failure.

The *side-cast reel* is a combination of all three previously mentioned reels. It has the large spool and direct-drive feature of the centre-pin; because the spool can be swivelled to face the rod tip for casting purposes it resembles the fixed-spool reel; and some side-cast reels have a star drag, a feature borrowed from the multiplier.

These reels are efficient and find considerable favour

5 The use of an 'educated thumb' is frequently more efficient than relying entirely upon the drag mechanism when playing a large fish

6 Beach angler using a side-cast reel. After casting, the reel is swivelled through 90 degrees for working the bait, playing the fish and recovering the line

among a wide section of sea anglers, both shore and boat enthusiasts. Naturally, when line is being recovered the spool is turned into the 'in line' position.

Whatever reel you choose, it is always important to equip it with the correct amount of line and not only the correct amount, but a line suited to the particular reel. The centre-pin design will accept either braided or nylon monofilament, and it should be remembered that it is pointless to put small amounts of line onto a large reel or to try and overfill a small reel.

Remember that while fishing at sea you may have 100 or 150ft of water beneath your keel. Add to this the distance the tide will carry your tackle, and the possibility that a big fish may demand 100ft or maybe more on its first run. You will see that anything less than 3–400ft of line would be totally unreasonable.

Fixed-spool reels were designed and came into use long before the advent of nylon monofilament line; but they never achieved popularity nor realised their full potential until monofilament line was invented. It is now accepted that the only line which operates satisfactorily with a fixed-spool reel is nylon monofilament, so use it; and fill the spool correctly with line of an adequate breaking strain. You will normally find that 20 or 25lb BS line is perfectly adequate with the average fixed-spool reel designed for seawater use. Always fill the spool to within one-sixteenth of its lip—this makes casting easier and ensures that you have an adequate supply of line.

Both braided and nylon monofilament can be used on multiplying reels, but remember the crushing effect that stretched nylon monofilament can have. When recovering line, particularly if a considerable amount has been out, make sure that it is spread evenly across the whole face of the spool as it is recovered. Use the thumb and forefinger of the hand supporting the rod; this hand is usually placed around the rod butt just above the fixing position.

7 When several are fishing together from the same boat, it is possible to keep the lines apart by altering lead weights, the lightest lead being fished from the stern, the heaviest from the more forward position

8 When fighting a heavy fish, use a pumping action to recover line. Reel in as you lower the rod tip and then hold as you gradually lift to an almost upright position before repeating the action

Finally, look after all your equipment, reels included. Salt water is an extremely corrosive element, capable of completely ruining, in a very short space of time, any item not designed for use at sea. Always make sure that any reel you buy conforms to the necessary specifications and never put it away soaked with seawater.

Rods

Most rods used for sea fishing are made of glass fibre. This term is not strictly correct as there are many other ingredients, but for all that it is still the term which is in general usage and one which is readily understood.

A high quality, solid-glass rod is extremely strong and almost indestructable and if it is to be roughly treated (and probably trodden on by young and careless feet) then it will fit the bill admirably. But there is certainly far greater pleasure to be derived from using the more sophisticated hollow-glass rod; it has a far sweeter action, it is lighter, and (weight for weight) much more powerful.

The intricacies of beach casting form a vast subject, way beyond the scope of this book. Here we are basically concerned with rods suited to fishing from boats or from various points along the shore where long casting is neither necessary, nor, in many cases, practical.

All rods have differing lengths and thicknesses; they all have handles (cork, wood or plastic), and rings to guide the line from the reel to the tip of the rod. They also have fittings on the butt end to attach and release the reel; and they can be made either in one piece or in connecting 'joints' or sections.

Limit yourself to a couple of rods; one designed to cast light lures and handle species such as mackerel, possibly bream and even one or two of the smaller flatfish, such as plaice and flounder, and a more robust boat rod.

The Falmouth-based Intrepid tackle company produces an excellent all-purpose spinning and light bottom-fishing or 'ledgering' rod. It is hollow glass with a plastic handle, and is in every way (including price) the type of rod which will serve the occasional angler extremely well. With a rod of this type you can fish quite efficiently in a variety of ways, as well as using many of the tackle assemblies explained later.

When considering a more sturdy boat rod there is the solid-glass range offered by the Shakespeare Company, both inexpensive and robust; or any one of a number of very adequate hollow-glass rods which can be found in any good tackle shop. Never hesitate to ask for advice: you will rarely save money by shopping around in supermarkets and multiple stores and, even if you do save a few pence, there is no substitute for the fund of knowledge possessed by the tackle dealer.

However, it is as well to be armed with one or two basic facts. For example, all rods should be equipped with an adequate number of rings, as the rod will snap more easily if insufficient rings are used. When the rod is under strain and the tip pulled round to a point approximately at right angles to the butt, the line should still be following the curve adopted by the rod. It should never touch the rod, or pass

9 Rod under strain—note how the rings carry the line, keeping it clear of the rod

Fig 3 A, Rod tip with a single roller ring
B, Double roller

from ring to ring across a line lower than the curve of the rod. (That is assuming that a reel is being used in the 'on top' position, see Plate 9.)

Make sure that the rod you choose is fitted with rings that match the type of reel you intend using. For example, a boat rod may have a single-roller top ring. A roller is designed to assist the rod and to enable line to be recovered more easily while playing a heavy fish. But a single-roller end ring is designed to be used with a reel which is fixed and used on the underside of the rod. If a multiplier were used, placed in the 'on top' position, the line would not run across the roller and could well be damaged by a part of the rod ring which was never designed to have line running across it.

If the rod is equipped with a roller-type top ring, make absolutely certain that it is a double roller if a multiplier is going to be used. Then the line is taken between the two rollers and will always be passing over a surface designed to accept the line. A rod with a double roller top ring can be used with either a multiplier or a centre-pin reel, as no matter which way the rod is turned the top ring will work correctly.

The rod's hand grip is also important. Occasionally rods are equipped with hand grips which are constructed and placed on the rod in such a way that the rod can only be fished comfortably in one position. These grips are grooved so that fingers fall into the slots. If these are fitted so that the rod rings must be uppermost when the rod is in use, use a multiplier, not an open faced fixed-spool or a centre-pin reel, both of which are fitted *under* the rod.

These are small points, but they can lead to a lot of annoyance if an unmatched rod and reel are chosen. When in doubt, consult the specialist tackle dealer.

Rods designed to be used with either a side-cast or fixed-spool reel should have a bottom ring designed to operate with this particular type of reel. As the line pays off the spool it is spiralling, and the distance across the spiral could be 2in or more. If the bottom ring is too narrow the line will be channelled too quickly into a straight line, and can therefore either catch around the ring or suffer friction damage. Thus a rod designed for use with a fixed-spool reel should have a relatively large bottom ring. This also applies when using a side-cast reel, as when the terminal tackle is cast the line is drawn from the side-cast reel in a way similar to a fixed-spool reel.

The relationship between rod, reel and line is highly important. If a very powerful rod is used, then it is ridiculous to use a light line and a small reel—when you strike at a fish the weight and power of the rod will merely snap the line. Conversely, if you have a very heavy line and massive reel on a light spinning rod, then it is almost an odds-on certainty that sooner or later the rod will be broken.

Generally speaking, assume that a spinning rod designed to cast a 1oz weight (including both lead and bait) will accept a line of around 12lb BS. Moving up into a slightly heavier class where weights of around 2oz are being used, a line of some 18lb BS would prove adequate, while in the 4–8oz weight bracket the angler should be using line of between 25 and 40lb BS. Matched tackle is therefore essential for *all* items of equipment: hook, line, weights, rod and reel.

Leads, wirework, and miscellaneous items

Leads enable a fisherman to offer a bait to fish on the sea bed. To do this they must be large enough not only to take the bait down to the bottom, but also to counteract the pull of the tide as it washes past the line. Strong or thick line will need a bigger lead than one of less bulky proportions, because it offers a greater surface area to the pull of the current. Braided line offers even more resistance to the tide, as line of this type tends to be bulkier than monofilament line of similar strength.

Therefore, if you want to fish from the moment the tide begins to make until it is full, you should use leads of varying weight to counteract its changing strength.

You will find that when using a monofilament line of approximately 15lb BS you need only use as little as 1oz of lead when fishing certain periods of a neap tide, while 4 or 6oz could be needed to do the same job when fishing at the same place during the full run of a spring tide.

You should therefore select a range of 4 or 5 bomb-shaped leads ranging from 1–4oz; a further 2 or 3 grip leads ranging from 3–6oz, and possibly a couple of heavy sinkers, for example one at 8oz and one at 1lb. These would be perfectly adequate for most situations. Your own experience plus advice from local tackle dealers will soon tell you if you need one or two more leads of various types.

While on the subject of weights, do not overlook *trolling*

10 A variety of leads, ranging from those which are anchor-like in their operation to those designed to roll over the sea bed or to be used as an added weight when spinning

11 A net is essential when sea fishing. Always play the fish to the net, never chase the fish, that is a sure way to lose it

paravanes. These are made of plastic and are extremely light and most efficient. They are particularly useful to the cruising and sailing man as they can be employed to fish a line of feathers, a spinner, or indeed virtually any lure which is designed to attract fish such as bass, mackerel and pollack.

Paravanes enable you to fish at a predetermined depth and angle away from your craft. A paravane has two sets of fixing points, one set being designed to accept the towing line. By changing its position, the paravane can be set to fish deep or shallow and, depending on the position of the lures, it will swing away to either port or starboard, or travel directly astern of your craft. There is one particularly useful aspect of trolling a paravane: as soon as the balance is upset by a fish taking the bait it will immediately draw the fish to the surface.

An enormous number and variety of snaps, buckles, quick-release attachments, Kilmore booms, paternosters and various other items of wirework will enable you to assemble all manner of tackle arrangements. It is virtually impossible to assemble a fishing rig without using one or two of them. The amount and variety required need not be excessive, but do not use swivels and buckles which are completely out of keeping with the remainder of your equipment. In other words, swivels designed for shark-fishing tackle should not be used to assemble a simple ledger rig on which you intend catching plaice or flounder. As a basic guide, work to the simple adage—'if it *looks* right then it *is* right'.

With luck, and a great deal of patience, the end result of assembling your hooks, line, weights, rod and reel should be

12 The confines of a small boat make snarled or scattered tackle a nightmare—neat, safe stowage is a must

the capture of a fish, and depending on its size you may need either a gaff or a net to get it on board.

Rods and reels are not designed to be used as cranes and winches. If you try to lift a heavy fish on a light rod you will almost certainly end up by breaking the rod. An efficient net is not an expensive item, and gaffs can either be made or bought for a pound or so.

Storing your tackle

Storing the many smaller items of equipment can be a headache, particularly in the confined space offered by some craft. Loose hooks can be extremely dangerous, and a dozen or so ruined buckles and swivels can add up to a couple of pounds or so—a not inconsiderable sum for a few relatively small pieces of tackle.

Tin boxes are never suitable storage containers, particularly when sea water is involved. Junk shops frequently yield an odd wooden drawer, or a box which can be adapted in one way or another. I have seen more than one excellent tackle box made from just a large wooden drawer. Polythene storage boxes are also excellent—the lids close tight, they are cheap and are unaffected by salt and damp. A block of expanded polystyrene, or a few old bottle corks, can be used to hold loose or spare hooks. Rods and gaffs can be placed in clips under a thwart, but stowing the items already discussed does not create the sort of problems raised by the equipment described in the next chapter.

4 Laying a Trotline

What is a trotline?

From orthodox rod and line fishing we now turn to some of the many ways developed by commercial fishing interests. These methods, if adapted and modified slightly, can be used by the boating enthusiast and yachtsman, and the financial outlay on equipment need not be particularly heavy.

One of the simplest methods is called *trotlining* or *longlining*, a name derived from the type of equipment used by professional fishermen in many parts of the world. A longline can be laid 'dry'—set on the foreshore while the tide is out—or it can be laid from a boat.

This piece of equipment has a number of names: 'longline', 'trotline', 'lay-line', 'set line' or any one of several other descriptions, many of which are purely local in usage. But the article itself is basically the same: a *backline* to which are attached *snoods*, short lengths of a much lighter line carrying the hooks.

The backline should be of a strength and size suited to the type of fish likely to be caught in the area being fished. Generally speaking, for inshore work, a line of about ½in circumference and made of Terylene or nylon is perfectly adequate. What is termed 'cod line' is ideal for this purpose. The use of a braided line for either the backline or snoods is not recommended, as many problems may arise as a result of the hook fouling the line.

Fig 4 Basic trotline dimensions, showing arrangement of snoods

Apart from this it is vital to use an extremely supple line for the snoods. One which is stiff and difficult to manage does not 'fish' particularly well; the bait presentation is all wrong.

The snoods are fixed at regular intervals along the line; for example, 16in–long snoods could be fixed every 3ft, and ideally they should be of approximately 40lb breaking strain.

The type of hook to use on a longline is always a matter for some debate. There are those who favour the rather cheap, tinned, whiting-hooks, but I would always choose the more durable stainless-steel variety. Tinned whiting-hooks are frequently soft and have a tendency to rust very quickly. If you want a carefully constructed trotline that will last for many years, remember that it is a false economy to use anything but a high quality hook.

A size 1/0 hook, in stainless steel, is the most convenient, and will hold most bait forms perfectly adequately.

Setting at low tide

It frequently pays to make up a trotline system employing a series of lines, each having twenty-five snoods and hooks. Thus a 100-hook line could be in four sections, each section of backline having an eye spliced into each end. This makes it very simple to set a short section of line in a restricted area. To lay a 100-hook line, each section is joined by slipping one loop through another and tying a half-hitch.

Trotlines can be set along the foreshore, on any suitable bank, or in a gulley—wherever the fish can reasonably be expected to feed. Lines set 'dry' at low tide should be laid parallel with the tide line. If there is a slight slope, this will help keep the hooks clear of the backline while the tide is flowing. It is very unwise to set a line at right angles to the tide flow as the pull of tide and weed can exert enormous strain.

Lines set at low tide must be watched until they are covered, and cleared as soon as the tide recedes. However, before you set a trotline on any stretch of foreshore, make absolutely certain you are not contravening local byelaws or regulations controlling the use of this type of equipment.

In some areas byelaws made under Section 82 of the Public Health Acts Amendment Act (1907) regulate the placing of fish hooks and metal stakes on the seashore. It may well be that a local authority will ban the use of trotlines for certain periods of each year, usually between April and October.

When laying a trotline along the foreshore, certain problems arise if the full 100 hooks are used on one continuous length. Fixing the ends is relatively simple and a good anchorage can be achieved in a number of ways, but if 100 hooks on approximately 320ft of line are laid, and the line is only fixed at its ends, there will be quite an amount of 'give' in the centre and this can cause problems.

Various methods can be used for securing the line at either end. Some may use a large stone buried in sand, or a small anchor. Even a metal bucket can be employed, sunk into the sand, as this can prove almost impossible to move. Good as these methods are, do not forget the problem of transporting weighty objects onto the foreshore, or of finding them there after you have arrived.

An excellent way to fix trotlines very efficiently (not only at both ends but also at one or more points in between) is with 6in squares of wood. Possibly the most easily obtained is a square of floorboard, but choose the section carefully, and avoid splits.

Drill a hole right in the centre of each square, put the line through the hole and knot it, then fix the line with a couple of staples for added security.

Bury the first square about 12in below the surface, and then bury the others at distances along the line—it is wise to use an anchorage point after every twenty-five hooks.

When laying a line along the foreshore, remember shrinkage. This does not arise with a line constructed of manmade fibre, but natural fibres will shrink somewhat when immersed in water. This could either cause a break, or force the anchors out of position. So never fully tighten a natural-fibre layline until it has become well soaked.

Sometimes the advancing tide will bring a line of weed with it. This could well smother the baited hooks before the fish have a chance to see them. If there are two or more of you engaged in setting the line, it is possible to hold the hooks clear of the first run of the tide, but it is better to cover each bait with a thin layer of sand. The baits will soon wash free, but by this time the weed will have passed and your baits should fish quite adequately.

With all such operations, experience is the best teacher. Varying tidal conditions and other local factors all have a bearing on the way in which you operate a layline. Take these into consideration and you should find this a most profitable way of fishing for fun.

Some beaches have a short, but fairly steep, slope and then a wide expanse, possibly 2–300yd of sandy or muddy foreshore, which is left exposed at low water. A foreshore such as this can be fished for quite a considerable period while the tide is coming in, the fisherman continually laying, lifting and clearing twenty-five-hook lengths of trotline.

The method is quite simple but does need a fair amount of

13 A longline, baited-up and ready for laying, with the baited snoods carefully arranged to avoid fouling as the backline is paid out

agility, and without doubt a considerable amount of fairly hard work is involved. Rhythm is the secret. Bait twenty-five hooks and weight the seaward end of the line with a large stone. Take the stone as far out to sea as you can wade. Drop the stone and pay out the hooks as you wade back towards the beach. When the last hook is laid, attach a length of line to the loop at the end and bring the spare line back onto the foreshore, some feet clear of the advancing tide line. Tie it to a bamboo pole or similar suitable stake driven into the shingle or sandy beach.

Repeat the operation with another twenty-five hooks some fifty or so yards from the first line, with another twenty-five hooks laid a similar distance away. This can be repeated so that you are operating three, four or even five short lengths of trotline.

As soon as the last line is laid, and the tide has reached the pole marking the end of the first line, it is time for it to be re-covered. Haul away and draw the line in; clean, clear and rebait; then wade out and drop the stone at a point which you can safely reach. (Needless to say this is going to be that much further inshore than the point you reached when you began.) Then repeat the cycle with the other lines. Just how many times this can be repeated depends upon the avail-ability of the bait, the speed at which the tide is travelling and other similar factors.

Finally, you might consider operating one or more trot-

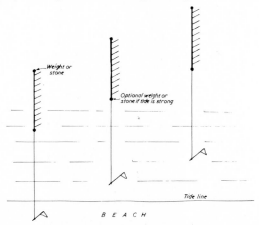

Fig 5 Setting three trotlines as the tide makes

lines through pulleys. The equipment for this can vary from nothing more complicated than a galvanised metal bucket set into the sand, the handle being left free, or a couple of pulley wheels (galvanised of course) fastened to stakes well set into the sea bed.

Fasten one end of the line to a stake high above the high-water mark. Take out the line at right angles to the beach, run it through a pulley and then back to the shore to a point some 20–30ft away from the other end of the line which has already been fixed to a stake. Your trotline is then fixed to either end of the line, baited, and is then drawn out to sea by hauling on the end of the line which is not fixed to the trot-line. If a mark is made on the original hauling line at the point where it goes through the pulley you will know exactly when your backline has reached the pulley or bucket handle, or whatever is being used as a seaward end mark.

Storing trotlines

The trotline itself should be stored in a suitable container and coiled into the box in reverse—in other words, the last section of the line to go in is the first section to be layed.

The container in which the line is placed is usually called a 'trot box'. The line is coiled into the box and the hooks are layed over the edge, sometimes into a V-shaped notch or into saw cuts. These notches or cuts keep the snoods in order and help to prevent them from becoming tangled.

Trotting from boats

Shooting or laying a trotline from a boat is more difficult, and certainly trickier. Safety first: remember not to wear a loose or flapping coat, a floppy jersey or any item of ex-tremely loose clothing in which hooks can catch.

Always have a sharp knife ready to hand, for if a hook should snag either the boat, or, worse still, an arm or hand, it is vital for the snood to be cut quickly. If it is not, the whole weight of both line and boat comes on the victim. This may

sound melodramatic but it is wise to take the necessary pre-
cautions before you start.

When laying a trotline in the open sea it is customary to
use either an anchor, cinch, or other suitable weight to secure
it to the bottom. Under normal conditions, a 7lb fisherman's
anchor is adequate for an operation of this type, but a
cinch—and this is usually no more than a bunch of old
chain—should weigh approximately 14lb or more if it is to
be efficient. The weight or anchor should never be tied
directly to the end of the trotline as this would cause diffi-
culties when hauling the line or letting go the tail end of it
when laying.

Remember that, although thin lines may be strong enough
to perform the task in question, it is always more difficult to
handle a thin line than a thick one. Therefore, when weights
are involved, such as lifting an anchor, it is always considerably easier (and your hands are less likely to be
damaged) if you use a more bulky line.

You *must* use an additional length of much heavier line at
both ends of the trotline. The length of this extra line should
be slightly more than the maximum depth of the water in
which the trotline is being laid. You can then lower the
anchor or weight right to the bottom before you have to start
paying out the backline.

You must also mark both ends of the trotline with a marker
of one sort or another. A small marker buoy, or even a line of
corks similar to those used by lobster fishermen, can be used,
but remember that a line of corks can be hard to see. In a
slight chop or swell corks are almost invisible to the naked
eye until you are virtually on top of them. Even a brightly
coloured marker buoy, unless sufficiently large, can be
equally difficult to see.

Making a marker flag

A marker flag is best, and you can make one quite easily. All
you need is a broom pole, a small amount of sheet lead and a

few squares of cork or expanded polystyrene.

Punch a hole in the centre of the cork or polystyrene and place a 3ft length of broom handle through the hole. Make it a very tight fit and it will stay in place. Wrap an amount of lead around one end of the pole and fix a flag to the other. With sufficient lead the pole will float upright, and this can be seen for a considerable distance. Drill a hole through the pole just above the lead and splice a loop of line for fixing purposes. A line then runs from this loop down to the weight or anchor. Remember to use a strong line: this is the line which you will use to lift the anchor holding the trotline in position.

Put special identifying marks on each flag so that each end of the line is recognisable. This could be important if the trotline were to be broken for one reason or another.

Laying line from the boat

When shooting a trotline, lay it over the starboard side of the boat in relatively slack water, or when there is just sufficient tidal movement or wind to take the boat away in the direction of the main tidal run. The line should be laid while the boat is moving slowly; this gives the operator enough time to clear any small snags which may arise despite the best of preparations. The line and baits should have been placed in the box in the correct order and everything arranged well in advance.

Put the anchor or weight over the side first, then pay out the two lines, one to the marker flag and one to the trotline. As soon as the anchor has taken a grip, begin laying the line. Clear away the remainder of the line which is attached to the marker flag, and, as the tide carries you slowly away, lay the line tightly and evenly across the sea bed.

As you reach the end of the trotline, hold for a moment or two to straighten the line right out, and pay out the remainder to the second weight or anchor and finally the marker flag and line.

A trotline is normally left in position until the tide has run its course, but it can be picked up against a much slackened flow. In other words, if the line were laid just after high water, it could be picked up just before low water slack. However, local tidal conditions, and the fact that neap tides may be running, could greatly facilitate the laying or picking up of such lines. Trotlines shot overnight onto a sandy bed will often bring good catches of sole, but such fishing can demand a very early start.

Recovering the line

When picking up a trotline, approach the downtide float-line first and bring the float inboard over the starboard side of the boat, hauling it in rapidly as the boat is turned slightly off course. By positioning the boat in this way it will tend to 'belly' the trotline as it is hauled in, while by keeping the boat moving slowly ahead into the tide run you can haul in the line at a measured rate, the boat keeping pace with the rate of line recovery. This manoeuvre will also keep the hull away from the main line of hooks and fish.

As soon as the floatline, weight and first section of the hauling line come aboard, they should be coiled down very

Fig 6 Suggested methods for recovering trotline laid in open sea to keep the line away from the propellor: A, approaching pick up mark; B, picking up and clearing lay-line

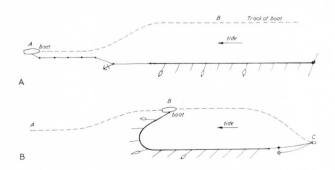

rapidly and kept out of the way of the main trotline.

Immediately the first of the backline and hooks come aboard, they should be coiled down onto the deck as evenly as possible, depending on the amount of weed, or the speed at which the line is being hauled onto the deck.

As each fish comes over the side, swing it clear of the main coil of line and, if it is a large fish, such as a skate, ray or conger eel, cut the snood as it comes over the side and throw the fish clear.

It is surprising how little tangle can result if this method is followed, providing the fish are left undisturbed. Bear in mind that they may have been hooked for many hours before being hauled to the surface, and therefore will have become virtually exhausted before being brought up.

After detaching the hauling line the trotline should be coiled back into the box, the snoods made safe and the hooks cleared of all weed and rubbish.

For storing and transporting a trotline which is used from a boat, you would do well to imitate the professionals who use a special type of box, designed to accommodate the line and to enable the angler to bait the hook and shoot the line from a moving craft with comparative ease.

The box is designed so that the baited hooks can be laid in the front section in the reverse order to which they are paid out. This cuts down the risk of a tangle of hooks, snood and backline.

The box can also be used for storing the line when not in

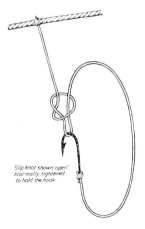

Slip knot shown 'open'. Normally tightened to hold the hook

Fig 7 Safety first: how to backhitch snood hooks

use; and it is while the line is being stored that it can become somewhat muddled. To reduce this possibility a method known as 'back hitching' is used, which, despite its somewhat obscure name, is really quite a simple method.

Form a slip knot in the snood, as close to the backline as possible, lay the bend of the hook into the loop of the slip knot and tighten the knot until it is just—and no more than just—holding the hook in position. Hooks stored in this way are as safe as it is possible to make them. In fact when they are back hitched you can run your hand down the backline and the hooks will not stick into your hand: they will only present the bottom of their bends, and your hand will slide over them in complete safety.

Occasionally a strip of cork is nailed along the back of the trot box and the hooks stuck into this soft material. But if you use a trot box of this kind you must have two boxes, so that the line can be fed from one, baited, and then laid into the second. This is not as efficient as back hitching the hooks, as then the whole trot can be lifted out of the box and coiled back in as it is baited.

It is always difficult to estimate the number of fish likely to be taken on a trotline. Crabs, whelks, and small fish are likely to attack the baits before the fish you hope to catch are hooked. And even when fish are caught it is always possible that a large predator, such as a conger eel or tope, may come along and neatly bite off the body of those fish that you have hooked, leaving you with no more than a dozen or so heads decorating a 100-hook trotline.

Laying short lines

A trotline of twenty to thirty hooks can be fished from an anchored boat and quite reasonable hauls can be achieved. There is a simple but effective method of getting twenty or more hooks a sufficient distance from your boat, and at the same time laying them neatly onto the sea bed.

A wine bottle, a very porous floor cloth, or even an old tin can will serve for this. Attach it to a length of light line—10 or even 15ft—then fix the end of the light line to the end of your trotline. The wine bottle goes over the side and is allowed to float away downtide, taking with it the light line, followed by the baited hooks. When the last hook goes over the side allow a further 15 or 20ft of line to go away on the tide, and at this point attach a weight, sufficient to carry all the hooks to the bottom. A few jerks on the line and the wine bottle will tilt, fill with water and sink. Lower the weight and your trotline will be laid neatly on the sea bed.

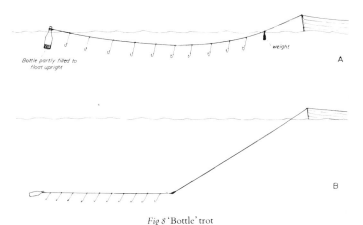

Bottle partly filled to
float upright

A

B

Fig 8 'Bottle' trot

5 Choosing and Storing Bait

The collection of natural bait and its storage are an essential part of fishing. The chances of making a good catch are much reduced unless you have enough bait which is also of high quality. Poor quality tackle with good bait will catch more fish than high quality tackle with poor bait.

Remember that many species of fish not only have poor eyesight, but are also living in a world which, for a variety of reasons, may present them with a medium through which it is difficult to see, and more often than not vibration serves as the first attraction.

The second attraction is smell. A fillet cut from a freshly killed mackerel is probably one of the most deadly baits that can be used. The oil and juices of the flesh drift away on the current, and hunting fish very soon pick up the scent and follow the trail to its source.

Almost as deadly is a 'rubby dubby'—a sack or bag made of small-mesh net and filled with minced fish offal mixed with bran and soaked with pilchard oil. The bag is either lowered to the bottom on a weighted line, or hung over the bows so that the rise and fall of the craft will continually dip the bag into the sea. This action results in particles being washed out to float away on the tide.

Artificial bait

Artificial lures have, in recent years, become far more widely used. To some extent this is because of the eternal difficulty in getting bait at short notice. Not all tackle shops sell bait, and in any case the boat owner may well launch his craft in an area where bait is just not available. In this case you must either collect your own or use artificial lures.

Artificial lures imitate the movements of small fish and

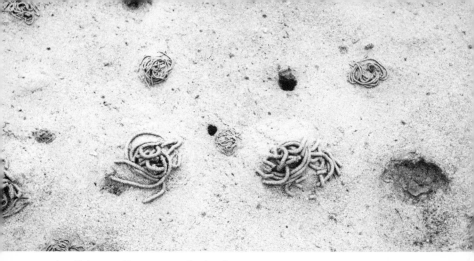

14 The telltale signs of lugworm in sand and mud

other creatures upon which predatory fish live. They are
normally made of plastic, wood, metal or feathers, and spin
or wobble as they are drawn through the water. This movement sets up vibrations, and the multi-coloured or shiny sides
flash with reflected light.

For the boat owner who only fishes occasionally, a selection of lures are most worthwhile items to have on board.
But use them sensibly! They are not designed to catch fish by
being left lying motionless on the sea bed. They must be

15 Nothing destroys a good worm bed faster than leaving it full of crater-like excavations.
For the worms' sake and also for the sake of future anglers, fill in as you go

given movement by the fisherman, and operated in such a way that they will attract predatory fish. This is of course not the case when one is fishing with natural baits, as these usually have their own 'inbuilt' attractions.

Natural Baits

Worms

The common *lugworm* is probably the most useful and easily obtained marine worm used as bait. You can often buy them in tackle shops, but remember that seasonable demands can regulate supplies. A sandy or muddy foreshore suits these creatures, and their existence is denoted by what is known as a 'cast'. These sandy extrusions, rather like a thin piping of sandy 'icing sugar', mark one end of a U-shaped tube in which the lugworm lives. At the other end of the hole there is a small depression, which is frequently—but not always—on the seaward side of the cast.

Lugworms vary in colour and size, depending on the habitat from which they are taken. The average lugworm is about 6–8in long. Its body could be described as being in two sections. The forward end is the thickest and contains its body mechanism, and also has some bristles along the sides. The rear section is really no more than a long cylinder of skin packed with sandy waste from which the creature has extracted food.

Collecting lugworms is relatively simple, but it does entail a fair amount of work. They are dug with a flat-bladed fork and, depending upon the number of worm casts, you can either dig them singly or take out a trench as one would when digging the garden.

Always replace all the disturbed mud and sand. To leave an area of foreshore looking like a bomb-cratered battlefield is not only a sign that an amateur has been at work, but the legacy of holes can be dangerous to youngsters paddling. Careless digging also ruins a bait-bed extremely quickly.

As a direct result of indiscriminate bait digging, some local authorities have begun instituting restrictions of one kind or another. So before you start to dig, always make sure that you are not breaking any local byelaws. Never disturb the bed near moorings or where boats are at anchor.

Lugworms should be collected in a suitable container of either plastic or wood, and always sorted as soon as you complete digging. Remove any dead or injured worms at once, as they will very quickly kill the others.

Lugworms keep extremely well in a shallow wooden box which has been well dampened with a small amount of the local sand. Place the worms evenly across the whole area of the box, and cover them with either seaweed or wet sacking. Only use seawater and sand from their natural habitat; freshwater will kill them.

In hot weather it is difficult to keep lugworms alive for more than twenty-four hours, and if they are left in the sun they will be dead within an hour or so. Always store them in a cool place, and always *keep them covered*.

Ragworms

The most common variety is the *king rag*—a segmented body with a fringe of hairs or bristles. They also have a small pair of pincers at the head which can give quite a sharp nip.

Ragworms can be as much as 15–18in long, but an 8–9in worm is more usual. They are generally found in creeks and harbours, particularly along the south coast of England, but this is not to say that they will never be found elsewhere. They are collected in much the same way as lugworms, but they are frequently found around and under large stones and boulders. In fact ragworms can be collected from the surface just under a boulder. But you must be quick, as they will disappear into the mud extremely quickly.

King ragworms tend to live fairly close to the low water mark of ordinary tides, but *white ragworms* are more often encountered when digging in the sand for lugworms. Some ragworms, and these are generally very soft, can be found in the upper section of shells occupied by hermit crabs.

Ragworms can be stored in much the same manner as lug-worms, but should never be mixed with them. The box containing mud or damp seaweed should be tilted so that any water drains down to one end.

Ragworms can be used in sections. They break apart quite easily, and you can obtain several baits out of one large worm. Always leave a small section trailing beyond the bend of the hook; as this moves in the current it becomes most attractive to fish. Very small ragworms are frequently more effective if hooked in bunches.

Shellfish baits

The *mussel* is probably one of the most easily found and useful shellfish baits, but it will not stand up to long casting, being a very soft-bodied creature. It can, however, be used quite efficiently by boat fishermen or where there is deep water close in and energetic casting is not essential.

To open a mussel which is going to be used for bait you need a sharp, thin-bladed knife. Insert this between the shells at the broad end, and without actually separating them, slip the knife blade right around both halves. The muscle just inside the shell's broad end must be severed so that the mussel will open completely on its natural hinge at the back. The flesh can then be scooped out and the hook placed through the brown- or purple-coloured foot which will be seen once the shell is opened. The remainder of the flesh is wound around the hook, and the whole bait is held in place by using a small section of the muscle or a small piece of worm or fish on the hook tip. Mussels are a good bait for many species of flatfish, as well as cod, codling, and bream.

Cockles can also be used as bait, particularly for flatfish. The cockle is somewhat tougher than the mussel, and should only be used as a standby bait if nothing more suitable is available.

Whelks are not particularly attractive to fish, but they have the advantage of being extremely tough. They can be used on trotlines during the winter months when other more attractive baits are in short supply. When using whelks as bait, remember to bring the hook right through the flesh and clear the barb. If this is not done the hook may not penetrate the fish's mouth.

The *common limpet* lives in a conical shell attached to rocks and concrete walls which are submerged at high tide. It can be dislodged from its position by a sharp tap with a stone or hammer, and the flesh cut out from the shell. The body is quite firm, and not easily stripped from the hook. These shellfish are not so readily acceptable to fish, but they can form a reasonably good bait for cod or bass, particularly during the winter months when food is scarce.

The *slipper limpet* is commonly found in clusters of seven or eight, each fixed to the back of the other, the base limpet possibly clinging to a stone to keep it secure. During heavy weather and high surf, many are washed up above the high water mark, where in summertime they open and die after being exposed to the sun. When they are subsequently washed back into the sea they attract fish right into the surf. Anglers who have taken advantage of these conditions have caught considerable bags of fish.

Although the slipper limpet itself is quite large in the shell, the amount of flesh is relatively small, and two or three may

16 Slipper limpets, stinking but irresistible to bass

be necessary on each hook. It is common practice to keep slipper limpets for a period until they become 'high'—they also tend to become slightly luminous, which may increase their attractiveness.

Razor fish are an extremely attractive bait for bass, plaice and other fish. They are generally found in the sand at low water mark when their presence is disclosed by jets of water spurting from the sand.

A good way to collect these is to pour coarse salt down their 'blowhole' to make them rise to the surface where they can be removed by slipping a spade underneath them. A more professional method, which needs some skill, uses an iron rod with a flattened, pointed end. This is thrust into the hole and into the open end of the shell. The razor fish, resenting this intrusion, clamps down on the end of the rod and can then be pulled out. In some areas where the sand is reasonably hard and the razor fish cannot rapidly go deeper, they can be dug from the sand like lugworms. After heavy weather, razor fish may also be found along the high water mark, having been swept from the sand by heavy surf and left high on the beach.

Clams and *piddocks* are other types of shellfish which may be particularly common towards the seaward end of estuaries and creeks. The shells are oval and the flesh can form a substantial bait, particularly for cod and whiting. They are an attractive bait as the flesh is colourful, with a bright orange-red roe, and they can be easily extracted from their shell. They can be obtained both from fishmongers and local fishermen in the area in which they are caught.

The collection of shellfish is not difficult, but storage may prove a problem particularly in hot weather. They can be kept in a sack or fine mesh net hung over the stern of the boat, or, alternatively, they can be dipped into the water once or twice a day for a few minutes to freshen them up. It is essential to keep them cool, and even a box covered with a wet sack is better than leaving them to dry out and die.

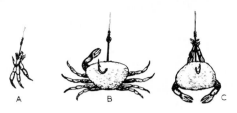

Fig 9 Three methods of using crab as bait: A, Crab legs; B, Soft crab with one claw removed; C, Soft crab with legs tied to hook shank

Crabs

Most fishermen probably think of crabs as thorough nuisances which rapidly strip the bait from a hook. However, all crabs go through a change during their life when they shed their shell so that they can grow, and at this time they are particularly attractive to predatory fish such as bass, the small, green, shore crabs making excellent bait. Crabs shed their hard outer covering as their bodies grow too large for the existing shell, which has to be discarded.

A crab due to shed its shell looks dull and lifeless, and is called a 'peeler'. The shell can be prised off with a fingernail, exposing a soft but leathery underskin. When the old shell is discarded the crab is known as a 'softback'. During the period it is waiting for the shell to harden it is completely defenceless, and therefore hides under rocks, pieces of stone and in old tin cans, etc. A peeler, or even a softback crab, may also be found clinging to the underside of a much larger hardback crab. Search through the pools and weed for bait of this type.

Both peeler and softback crabs are excellent baits for bass fishing along a shingle bar, at the entrance of a harbour, or in the surf. Remove one or two legs so that the hook can be inserted into the socket and then through part of the body. The remaining legs should be bound to the hook to prevent the bait tearing away. Additional fixing can be achieved by using a rubber band or elastic thread. Sometimes a treble hook is used, but the body of the crab tends to shield at least two of the points.

When collecting baits of this kind, bear in mind that soft-back and peeler crabs should be kept apart; both the hard-backs and peelers will eat those which have already shed their shells.

While searching rockpools, you may see an apparently discarded whelk shell which moves from time to time, and possibly shows a small claw or feeler at the opening. This shell has now become inhabited by a *hermit crab*, an excellent bait for bass or other large-mouthed fish such as cod or codling. The tail, when nipped off immediately to the rear of the body, forms an excellent bait for bream.

Hermit crabs can often be obtained in quantity from local lobster fishermen, or, alternatively, an old lobster pot laid on rough ground will often bring all you require. If kept in the sea they can be stored in a perforated box or an old lobster pot with a lid fitted over the entrance.

Fish baits

The majority of sea fish are cannibals, and therefore baits from such fish as *mackerel* and *herring* can be extremely productive. Mackerel, herring and *pilchard* have a high oil content and are particularly favoured as bait, as the oil coming from the flesh floats away down tide attracting the fish to the bait.

17 Filleting mackerel for bait. The 'last', or 'lask', is the triangular portion down by the tail

Mackerel, pilchard and herring can be used as bait in various ways, not only whole but also filleted or cut into strips of varying shapes, and one of the most popular sections of the mackerel is what is generally known as a 'lask' or 'last', cut from the tail end of the fish.

Fillets should be placed on the hook by inserting the tip into the skin side and out through the flesh; the bait is then twisted and the hook is pushed through again, skin side first. This method ensures that the maximum amount of flesh is

18 A splendid collection of sand eels collected by seine net. These are an excellent bass bait and can be kept alive in a courge or penner. The garfish is also excellent eating—ignore the green bones when cooked

shown, and allows the oils to ooze out into the water.

Small fish, for example *sprats* or even small *pouting* and *whiting*, can be used in a variety of ways. They may be hooked in bunches, or possibly singly, just through the flesh adjoining the tail fin.

When using a whole mackerel, slash its body along each flank. This enables the body juices to escape, which attract predatory fish.

Fig 10 A, a wicker courge; B, wooden penner. Both are ideal for storing sand eels, prawns, but if crabs are being held they must be fed and not overcrowded. Failure to observe the last rules will result in the crabs eating each other

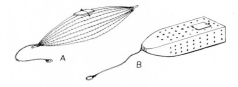

Sand eels

Sand eels are another extremely valuable bait. They are not easy to find; in fact they are probably one of the most hard-to-come-by baits used by the sea angler. Frozen eels are fairly widely available, but these tend to have lost much of their at-tractiveness to fish.

In some areas local fishermen specialise in collecting sand eels, using a net called a sand eel seine. If you should decide to invest in a net of this type, make absolutely certain that it is legal to use it where you intend fishing. It is a very fine-mesh net, and in some areas the use of such a device is illegal.

There are two types of sand eel, the greater and the lesser, but generally speaking the angler will be more concerned with the smaller variety which is some 4–5in in length. Sand eels can burrow into the sand very rapidly and so they can also be dug from the sand with a small handfork or scraped out with a wire hook.

Obviously both these methods are only successful in areas where sand eels are found in reasonable numbers. In the West Country, collecting eels with a hook is often called 'vingling', the eels are known as 'launce', and the wire hook a 'launce hook'.

Eels collected by this method normally do not live as long as those caught in a seine net. They are extremely delicate creatures, and should be handled as little as possible. Never leave them in the full glare of the sun, and put some weed in their container. Do not use metal containers such as galvanised pails, as the action of salt water on the metal is fatal to sand eels.

When fishing in slack water, sand eels can be hooked through the skin of the back, or through the gills and into the skin of the belly, but if there is any appreciable tide running they are best hooked by passing the hook through the eye, or through the lips. This is apparently irresistible to fish.

If the sand eel is freshly killed, or has been frozen, then placing the hook through the eye is probably the most satisfactory method. Hooked in this way the sand eel moves extremely well and forms a most enticing bait. Sand eels can be trailed behind a moving boat, or cast and retrieved as one would do with any type of artificial bait. They can also be fished as a dead bait on the bottom, and are also extremely attractive when used on long lines. If you own a deep freeze, a good supply of these creatures will never come amiss. But do remember that damaged or distorted sand eels are never so attractive to fish.

Cuttlefish and squid

During May and June cuttlefish are often seen floating on the surface of the water. Many of these will have lost their tentacles, possibly as a result of attacks by dogfish, tope or shark. Net them carefully and clean them in a bucket, but remember how messy these creatures can be. If you cut them open on the deck you can create a most appalling mess. Inside the body there is an ink sac, which if broken will flood the surrounding deck space with an oily black substance which will stain any unprotected wood.

However, they make extremely good bait; the flesh is tough and stays on the hook extremely well, and many fish, for example conger, skate and tope, will accept it readily. Strips of cuttle can be used to fish for bass, bream and various other species, and many anglers use small pieces of cuttle in conjunction with worm or mussel. You can also buy small squid from some fishmongers as well as from tackle shops. These make good baits, both whole or in sections.

Cuttlefish may be found washed up on the foreshore, but usually when they have been brought in by the tide they are half rotten and useless as bait.

Shrimps and prawns

Prawns are extremely good bait for fish and without doubt they are highly efficient, particularly when fishing for bass. But it can be a big problem to keep the baits alive, as a dead prawn or shrimp is nowhere near as efficient as a live one. Putting weed into the storage container helps. Any box or container which will keep the prawns or shrimps alive, but does not allow them to escape, will be perfectly adequate.

Always use a short-shank hook when fishing with prawns, and hook them through the last but one segment of the tail. Baits of this kind should not be fished on heavy tackle; the line

Fig 11 Prawns can be mounted singly (A) with the hook through the last but one segment of the tail, but as shrimps (B) are much smaller animals they are normally fished two or three to a hook

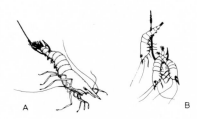

A   B

should be light, and the rod matched to it. This is necessary so that the movement of the prawn, even at a distance of 50 or 60yd, can be felt as the vibrations are transmitted down the line. As the prawn is allowed to drift downtide, it kicks or flicks its tail, and it is this movement which attracts fish. When a bass or similar predatory fish approaches the bait the kicking sensation increases rapidly as the prawn becomes agitated. This is a very good warning that the bait is about to be taken.

Both prawns and shrimps can be fished on float tackle if desired.

Other baits and home-made lures

In recent years artificial baits of all kinds have become more popular, but most of them tend to be quite expensive. Before spending large sums of money on these fascinating pieces of angling hardware it is worth while considering a number of alternatives.

Bacon rind is quite a good bait for both pollack and bass. Cut it so that it represents either a sand eel or a cuttlefish portion, and trail it behind a moving boat. Do not be afraid of leaving a small amount of fat on the rind.

If you search among the rocks at around the low water mark you may well find *anemones* of a type often referred to by professional fishermen as 'crasse'. These have a thick, firm flesh and are a dull, deep-red colour. They can be cut into sections and used to catch cod and other bottom-feeding fish.

Where professional fishermen operate it is often possible to get a supply of *skate* or *ray liver*. This is a good bait for a fairly wide range of fish.

Over the years many unusual baits have proved unexpectedly successful. For example, tripe and even sausages have caught fish, and there is absolutely no reason why various experiments with other off-beat baits should not be tried.

Possibly one of the most popular 'do it yourself' lures is the

19 Artificial squid. There's a tremendous range of artificial lures, but sometimes a crumpled milk-bottle top will prove as deadly to fish as any of them

artificial sand eel. Some professionally made models are highly efficient, and during the course of the year take many hundreds, if not thousands, of fish. The fisherman who is only moderately useful with his hands can make imitation sand eels with short lengths of rubber tubing and a few beads, a length of nylon, a hook and a twist of wire. The addition of a swivel and a split ring will make a near perfect artificial eel.

Visit a junk shop and buy a few old dessert spoons. It needs little imagination and even less skill to turn them into the type of 'spoon' used by anglers when fishing for flounders. You only have to look at the professionally made models to see how you can adapt a few old pieces of cutlery.

20 Unhooking mackerel caught on a string of simple feather lures. However, a line full of flapping mackerel, unguarded hooks and a heaving deck make a dangerous combination. Always take care when using tackle of this sort

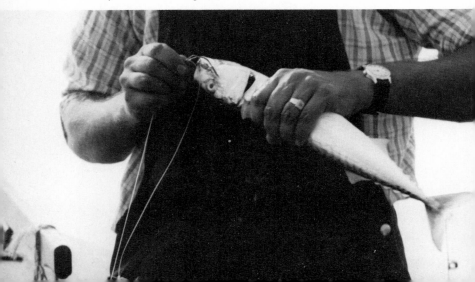

Sets of feathers are available at almost any tackle shop, and these can be used to catch mackerel, pollack, cod and codling. A set of feathers usually consists of twelve hooks, the feathers being whipped to the hook shanks, and each hook tied to a short length of stiff nylon snood which helps to stand the hooks clear of the backline. Feathers can be jigged or trailed behind a moving boat.

The Norwegians market an extremely efficient set of lures which consist of small plastic tubes, rather like 3in–long sand eels. These alternate with small single hook spoons and as lures, can be more effective than feathers.

A vast number of simple lures can be made quite cheaply. The aluminium foil from a milk bottle top, a strip of white rag, a fairly large rubber band, or even the silver paper from a cigarette packet can be used in varying situations, and all will catch fish at one time or another. A gull's feather floating on the surface of the water can be used. Bound onto the shank of a hook it can be trailed through the water where it may attract mackerel, bass or any one of a number of predatory species.

One of the most deadly of all the imitation sand eels is the very famous '*redgill*'. These are really excellent lures for a variety of predatory fish, but especially bass.

Another excellent professionally made item is the *mackerel spinner*, preferably mounted with a single spoon. The Toby spoon in silver or gilt, or any of the cuillers or bar spoons which have a wobbling action, all are well worth keeping on board.

Remember, you only need to catch one fish and you have a rich supply of bait. Both the flesh and the skin can be used, and a quick gutting operation may also provide several more baits, particularly if the fish you have just caught has been feeding on other small fish.

6 How to Catch Fish

Most fish, like people, tend to live in certain fairly well defined areas, and when they move they frequently do so as a group or shoal. This simple fact is frequently ignored by anglers, and as a result they fail to catch the fish they should.

At any given point fish stocks change from season to season, and this is why it is necessary to be able to employ a variety of techniques. Knowing how to assemble tackle and use it is not enough: you must also know where and when fish are likely to be available, and how to handle them when caught.

When considering the various locations and the species which may be found there, in conjunction with the methods which can be used to catch them, remember that there are very few clear cut lines of demarcation in the sea. For example, cod, a species normally associated with open water, may be caught several miles up the estuary of a tidal river, or even two or three miles from the entrance to a natural harbour such as Chichester or Portsmouth. Such catches add spice and excitement to a sport which is well known for surprises.

The areas which can probably offer most in the way of unpredictable fishing, and sometimes even an incredibly wide range of species, are natural harbours such as Chichester, Salcombe, the Tamar estuary, the Firth of Clyde and many similar places. While all do not hold the same species, each is an interesting fishery in its own right.

Sheltered waters, harbours and estuaries, offering as they do such a diversity of species, allow the fisherman to use a wide range of methods. In fact, apart from the highly specialised forms of angling such as hunting shark or giant halibut, virtually every method in the book can be tried at one time or another, always assuming that is, that conditions permit.

Fishing for flounder

One of the best examples of a species and location which can tax the angler's skill to the utmost is flounder-fishing in a sheltered tidal water, such as a natural harbour or fairly extensive estuary.

The flounder is a flatfish, one of several similar species which begin life as orthodox round fish like herring or cod. Before it reaches a length of about half an inch the flounder undergoes a complete change—its skull bones twist and one eye moves around its head so that both are on one side; the fish then adopts a side-swimming attitude.

Although the flounder is basically a bottom feeder, there are occasions when it will come up quite a distance from the sea bed, particularly when chasing small creatures which form part of its diet.

The flounder's food consists of small fish, shrimps and prawns, as well as crabs, various shellfish and marine worms—a fairly catholic diet. A flounder weighing around 4lb could be considered exceptional, one between 2 and 3lb is a good size, but a fish of less than $\frac{3}{4}$–1lb should be thrown back.

21 The flounder, one of the best known 'flatties'. These fish frequently have unpleasant skin eruptions and boil-like growths on their bodies. Any fish caught with these markings, usually caused by parasites, take ashore and bury—do not eat it!

Most flounders quit inshore waters around the turn of the year, returning during April or early May. Naturally there are both yearly and local variations to this pattern, temperature playing a big part in the timing of their seaward migration. Very cold weather will create a food shortage in shallow inshore areas; this in turn will send the flounders out that much earlier.

During the time it inhabits inshore waters, the flounder tends to be a shoal fish which moves with the current, feeding over mud and sand banks as it travels. Although they will come within a few yards of the shoreline where the beach is steep, they do not seem to like wide, flat expanses of mud or sand where the water is shallow and a falling tide rapidly leaves the bed uncovered. It also seems that flounders are attracted by movement—a crab shuffling across the sand, an eel burrowing into mud, or any one of a dozen or more similar activities.

Armed with this outline information it is possible to relate the knowledge of simple fishing techniques. The flounder's average size means that quite light equipment can be used, and also relatively small hooks, preferably of thin wire and with a long shank. Hooks of this type are ideal when used with worm bait. The thin wire helps penetration of the fish's mouth, and the long shank can make it easier to remove the hook after the fish has been caught.

As the flounder is basically a bottom-feeding fish, the angler must present his bait on or near the bottom, and knowing the type of food the creature is hunting makes it relatively simple for the fisherman to select the correct bait. For this, the simplest arrangement, and one which most anglers begin by using, is the *ledger*.

The Ledger

The lead, on a revolving spiral link, rests on a bead at the end of the line. Beyond the bead is a snap-link, to which is attached a 2-hook trace. It is possible to assemble a rig of this type with the minimum of equipment and can be fished perfectly adequately from a hand line. The hooks can be baited with lugworm, ragworm (king, red or white), small pieces of fish, or soft or peeler crab. These are the best bait for flounders.

There is one most important point to remember when assembling not only ledger tackle but all terminal rigs. Never use more weight than is necessary to achieve the desired result. In other words, if a 2oz lead will allow your tackle to fish correctly, use only 2oz, not 3 or 4oz.

When fishing for flounders remember that they will often investigate movement. Therefore, if fishing from a small craft, drift with the current, giving the occasional oar stroke to make your craft move just that much faster than the tide. When fishing from a boat which cannot be allowed to drift, add an amount of movement to the baited hooks by either casting away from your boat and slowly reeling in, or, if you are fishing with a hand line, slowly lifting the tackle every few seconds. The amount of movement in this latter case need not be very much: just a few inches is enough to arouse the flounder's curiosity.

Fig 12 Leger and two Flyers. This tackle arrangement, although more involved than many others, is extremely efficient. When tying the blood knot leave one 12in end, slip a 6in length of thin tube over it and pull the blood knot half way through. Tie the sea spoon judging the length of line carefully, when hook is secure, pull tube to cover hook eye. This should leave a tidy snood. The 2/0 Seamaster and Steelon trace is adequate for average size skate and ray etc. The two flyers will take cod, whiting and bream etc

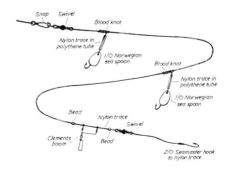

There is seldom any doubt that a flounder has taken the bait. When they are feeding well they bite quite fiercely, giving the rod tip a positive twitch. In fact, they will frequently give such a hearty pull that one can be forgiven for imagining the fish is a lot bigger than it really is.

Added movement can be given to ledger tackle by using a drilled bullet as a weight, and if this tackle is cast across the tide, the current will sweep it around. If a slow but steady recovery is made a considerable area of bed can be searched.

A most interesting method of fishing for flounders is by trolling a baited spoon. This will catch flounders when many other methods fail, but, although it is certainly the most efficient, it is not the easiest of methods to use. Not only is it essential for the tackle arrangement to be correctly weighted, conditions must also be in its favour. For example, a lot of floating weed will foul the hook and spoon and the tackle will become unusable.

It is also important for the arrangement to be correctly weighted. Too much lead and the spoon will plough through the mud, while too little weight will allow the hook to rise too close to the surface. My best catches have been made using a plain silver spoon between $2\frac{1}{2}$–3in long, with a hook set approximately its own length behind the blade. As always, local conditions have a great bearing on the type and size of spoon. Always seek advice on this subject either from local anglers or the local tackle shop.

Row with the tide, so that your increased speed will set the spoon blade revolving; this movement attracts the flounder which will in turn snap at the baited hook.

King rag is the best bait to use on spoons; lugworm is too soft and will very rapidly disintegrate when fished in this way. If lugworm is the only bait available do not hesitate to use it, but check your spoon more often.

If you are fishing by yourself, make sure that both oars are secured to your boat by lanyards, and that the rod is also made secure. A sudden bite may pull your rod over the side, or failing that you may lose your oars while attending to a fish. A sure indication that the spoon is 'working' is the steady pulse of the rod tip. Fish the spoon about 30–40yd astern of your boat.

Using float tackle

Float fishing

This is another interesting method, but it is a difficult technique when strong currents prevail. In some areas where both neap and spring tides produce powerful tidal conditions, float fishing can be extremely difficult if not impossible. However, there are places where even spring tides produce currents which make float fishing worthwhile. In other words, it is a matter of assessing the conditions prevailing at the point you are fishing, and deciding whether or not this method is practical.

A very strong current in deep water will mean that the bait is swept away long before the float has time to settle, and so much weight is needed to get the bait down to the fish that the whole exercise becomes impossible. However, where conditions allow, the use of 1–2oz of lead, and a slow but steady flow, draws the baited hook in a controlled way across the area to be fished, and then float fishing can be extremely productive.

You must allow for the speed at which the tide is either rising or falling. On a rising tide, within an hour of starting to fish, and assuming that you have set your depth correctly to start with, your bait could be 3ft higher in the water than when you started.

Let us assume that where you are fishing there is a 12ft tide. This means that the water will become 1ft deeper during the first hour, a further 2ft during the second, and 3ft during both the third and fourth hours. The rate of increase during the fifth and sixth hours would be approximately 2ft and 1ft, respectively. Obviously this is only an approximation, and various areas will have differing tidal conditions, but for all that the same basic considerations will apply.

Therefore, when commencing to fish with float tackle, make sure that the depth between the float stop and baited hook (see Fig 13) is roughly equal to the depth of water. After allowing for a certain amount of lift created by the tide flow, the bait will be approximately 2 or 3in above the sea bed.

Never allow more than ten or fifteen minutes to elapse between the times at which you check the depth of water, and reset your depth to equate with either a rising or falling tide.

There is an enormous range of floats, and a wealth of differing ideas regarding their use. I favour a cigar-shaped float as this shape does not offer an excessive amount of resistance to a taking fish. If the fish feels a lot of drag as it takes the bait, it will most probably reject the hook. One of the most important aspects of float fishing is the relationship between weight and float buoyancy. Use just enough lead to get your bait down to the required depth and to cock the float.

The amount of weight you use should almost, but not quite, equal the amount of buoyancy possessed by the float. If you achieve this happy balance, the slightest bite will be registered quite positively.

Float fishing is an ideal way of covering an extensive range of sea bed while fishing from an anchored craft. During the period the tide is making, the angler can cover a hundred yards or more on one side of the boat, and a similar area while the tide is ebbing.

Fig 13 Sliding float tackle. The float settles against bead and rubber stop and this controls the depth at which the bait is fished. Additional weight, Jardine spiral or fold over lead can be added to the trace if necessary

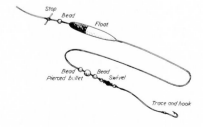

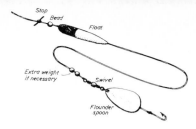

Fig 14 Float and spoon

Quite a wide variety of baits can be used on float tackle, in fact I have found both crab legs and peeler crab to be most effective during the period covering late spring and early summer.

Float and spoon arrangement

Many anglers favour a method which is really a combination of two previously described styles, with a spoon being float fished as well as trolled. Any of the accepted smaller flounder baits can be used, but personally I would present either king rag or lugworm when float fishing a baited spoon.

Fishing for bass

Another species which haunts a vast number of harbours, estuaries and other inshore waters is the bass. Its range extends from the Mediterranean to the British Isles, but as it has a distinct preference for warmer waters it does not seem to penetrate northwards much further than south-west Scotland on the Atlantic side, and the Lincolnshire coast in the east. Bass are common all around Ireland and, along the Causeway coast in the north, bass weighing 10lb and more are not uncommon. If flounders were to be described as sheeplike, then surely bass must be likened to wolves. While flounders forage quietly over mud and sand banks, bass go marauding across reef and harbour bar. They are magnificently equipped hunters: their great carpet-bag mouths spell death to myriads of smaller creatures every day. During the course of a tide, and depending upon availability, a 6–10lb bass may vary its diet by taking crabs, sand eels, and many other fish from inch-long fry to mackerel weighing a pound or more.

22 The sharp spines on the dorsal fin of a bass and also on its gill cover can cause an extremely painful wound

A shingle bar or reef running part way across the entrance to a harbour is often a favoured haunt of bass. Shoals of small fish, unable to swim against a powerful current, are congregated in a fairly tight-packed wedge of food as they are swept through the shallows. The bass need do no more than swim through the defenceless fry, mouth agape, feeding without effort.

By adapting the driftlining technique (Fig 15), you can take advantage of this natural situation. The hunting bass will be attacking and feeding quite freely and virtually any attractive object which comes into his range will be seized with an incredible ferocity.

Bass will stalk around jetties and piles, snapping up crabs they disturb in nooks and crannies. When conditions permit, they nudge and swirl through beds of bladderwrack and other weed, seeking creatures which have sought sanctuary there. These marine jungles can provide bass with shrimps, prawns, softback and peeler crab, not to mention the vast array of small fish which live in such surroundings.

Once again here is a situation which the fisherman can exploit. The keen fly fisherman may care to turn his attention to a fish which will take a fly in much the same way as a trout or salmon. Stalk your fish through the weed beds and watch for the telltale swirl of a bass feeding on insects and surface-born debris.

A light spinning rod, a fixed-spool reel and an assortment of lures makes an ideal outfit for hunting bass. This outfit can be used to fish for bass in a variety of situations. For example, a bass will forage along the tideline in no more water than it needs for it to swim. Crabs, small fish and marine worms flushed from the sand by the incoming waves, tumbling and beating on the shore, are all swept up and devoured. The fisherman can walk the tideline and systematically cast and search the close-in area of water.

Watch for the gulls

Seagulls often pinpoint the location of a number of bass. A squadron or two of shrieking gulls, circling and hawking, is a sure indication of carnage below. A wolf pack of hungry bass is, as likely as not, tearing through a concentrated mass of small fish.

Here again is a situation which the angler can exploit. By positioning a boat within casting distance of the main 'activity', a spinning technique will take fish, using a mounted sand eel. It may be possible to use the tide flow to get your bait working through the shoal of feeding fish. For example, if the boat is set into the tide run and the engine is operated to keep the boat on station, the angler can cast across the tide and, by checking the outrun of line, can swing the tackle back through the target area.

Trolling is another extremely effective technique, and one which can be used to catch not only bass but also mackerel

Fig 15 Driftlining technique and tackle. The exact and final composition of the terminal rig can only be decided when the conditions are known. With a strong tide and fish feeding deep, more lead would be necessary. With very little tide flow the tackle might be simplified to just a hook tied direct to the reel line

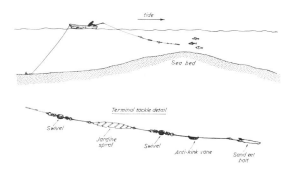

and garfish. Remember that a shoal of mackerel will frequently create the conditions already described. Mackerel
are great hunters who will also feed on small fish and, when
they do, the resulting activity by seabirds can lead the fisherman to believe that bass are causing the havoc. So do not be
surprised if mackerel take your bait.

When shooting a trolling rig there is always a danger of
fouling your propellor. It may be advisable to set your craft
into a shallow turn and pay out the baits and paravane over
the port side while turning to port, or vice versa.

Keep an open mind when fishing for bass. For example, in
a bay with a sandy shoreline at the centre, but where both

23 The gurnard, displaying the specialised pectoral fins which it uses to 'walk' on and cling
to the sea bed. Despite its appearance this fish makes excellent eating

24 The gurnard's profile, showing its angular head

ends terminate with a hard rocky headland, the headlands would not necessarily provide the most productive marks. Given good surf conditions and the knowledge that sand eels were found on that particular beach, you would expect bass to be hunting along the strand and not around the rocks. The raking surf would turn the eels from the sand, and in due course the bass would find them.

Similarly, in a harbour or estuary where channels divide sand or mud banks, instinct will tell the fish where food is most likely to be found. They might move station half a dozen times during a tide, but just where and when is something only experience and good local knowledge will reveal.

However, another method the fisherman might try, when drifting along channels and searching the odd corners from a boat, is to use a paternoster rig with an extra wide spreader. Bait this with sand eel on one side, king rag on the other.

Try a heavy metal lure . . .

The basic method is simplicity itself, but there are a number of variations. A very powerful rod with matching reel and line can be used to fish a very heavy metal lure. Lower this to the sea bed and jerk it erratically or steadily at varying depths, the method being open to infinite variation. In essence you are merely trying to attract the attentions of a predatory fish, one which will seize the lure, thinking it is a meal.

85

. . . or a feather-lure rig

At the other end of the scale you can use a dozen hooks dressed with feathers, (a standard mackerel lure), with half a pound of lead tied to one end and a length of cod line to the other. While drifting or moving slowly ahead under power, either lower the tackle until the lead strikes the bottom and then slowly recover, jerking the lures as you do so, or stream them behind your boat. Halfway between the two extremes, the rod and line fisherman may use any one of a score of more sophisticated and expensive lures, lowered to the sea bed and then jigged and danced at varying depths. Whichever you choose, you are merely attempting to lure a predatory fish.

Basically this method is one for the open sea, and the species which can be taken by this method include cod, ling, pollack, haddock and whiting. Naturally the method must coincide with the right time and place, and here local information is of the utmost value.

Pollack and ling

Quite a number of specialised cod lures are available these days, and an increasing number of really big cod, fish weighing 20lb and more, are caught each year on jigged lures. Although I have found this method to work best over rock and broken ground, many anglers have taken good catches of cod and whiting, whilst lure fishing over shingle, sand and mud.

Both ling and pollack tend to haunt rocky ground, but this is not an absolutely rigid pattern. Generally, ling are associated with wrecks, rocks and deep offshore water. As these fish are predators, and have powerful jaws well furnished with sharp teeth, when fishing for them, use a nylon-covered, steel trace. This trace must be strong (about 40lb BS should be adequate), and all swivels and links should be of matching size and strength.

Both pollack and ling, when brought up from depths of 30 fathoms or more, present a rather distressing picture. Their

25 The pollack has a big, thick-lipped mouth . . .

bodies are unable to accommodate the rapid change of pressure, and as a result you usually find their swimbladders protruding from their mouth—an unpleasant sight but unavoidable under the circumstances.

Haddock, cod and whiting

Haddock, cod and whiting are also taken on paternoster tackle; the hooks can be baited with worm, strips cut from other fish such as mackerel and herring, squid tentacles, and the various shellfish recommended for use as bait.

One of the most simple yet effective tackle arrangements for catching a wide variety of fish is the one in which you combine both paternoster and ledger, and, as if for good

26 . . . as does its cousin the cod. However they both make excellent eating and provide the sea angler with first-class sport

measure, incorporate a couple of Norwegian sea spoons, which are lures in their own right. (See Fig 12).

Although setting up this particular rig demands slightly more expertise, it is an extremely versatile arrangement. It is worth noting that on one occasion four of us, using similar rigs, while fishing off the Causeway Coast in the north of Ireland, caught cod, thornback, conger, gurnard, pouting, silver whiting, pollack, dogfish and a fine turbot. All these fish were caught from a boat drifting about a mile or so offshore.

The sea spoons can be baited with a wide variety of offerings, ranging from worm to strips of fish. Bait the bottom hook with an oily fillet cut from a herring, with possibly the head of a small squid on the lower flyer and worm on the upper. If fish are continually taken on one particular bait, try a similar bait on each hook.

When fishing a rig of this type from a drifting boat, remember to keep a very strict control over your line; if you fail to do this you will almost inevitably lose all the terminal tackle.

Preserving your tackle

Drifting over rock or broken ground calls for extreme care; it is so easy to get the weight trapped in a crevice. You may be well advised to tie the sinker to a length of relatively weak line, so that if the weight is snagged the link will break, thus saving most of your equipment.

27 The ling, a deep-water fish, and one which frequently reaches double-figure weights

Over very rough ground you may well prefer to experiment with a variety of weights ranging from gravel tied into a small square of thin rag, to an old bolt or two, or even a length of old motorcycle chain. If using the latter, make sure first that it is free from oil or grease.

As soon as the hooks are over the side, pay the line out gradually, and immediately the weight strikes bottom check the outflow of line and decide whether or not the amount of lead is sufficient to hold the baited hooks down while the boat is drifting. Too little weight and the tackle streams away close to the surface; too much lead will make it difficult to handle. It will lie too close under the boat, which can create problems when playing the fish and trying to land it.

I like to see the line laying away from the boat at an angle of about 40–45 degrees. As soon as the right 'set' has been achieved, fish the baited hooks 2–3ft up off the sea bed. Keep the bait moving up and down, and occasionally check the depth at which the hooks are fishing by paying out line until the weight strikes bottom, then reel in just enough line to ensure that the baits are the required distance from the bottom.

Whenever you hook a fish over rock, always make a point of regaining as much line as quickly as possible. If the fish is particularly lively, play it out at midwater, never close to the sea bed. A fish diving for cover can sever the line across a sharp edge of rock, or on jagged barnacles.

Coping with conger eels

One of the most violent and powerful fish that may be hooked while fishing over, or close to, rock is that formidable marine eel—the conger. If you bring one to the surface and decide to boat it, do so with care, particularly if it is a fish of some 20lb or more.

A conger has unbelievable strength, and one that has been hooked will almost certainly try to get its tail wrapped around a holdfast of one kind or another. If it succeeds, your chances of moving it from the bottom are indeed very slim. When a conger 'goes to ground' the options open to you are limited to a choice between a protracted tug of war, which may last several hours, or pulling hard on the line by hand until something gives—usually the line will snap at a knot, this being the weakest point.

However, assuming the conger is brought to the surface, on seeing it you must decide whether or not to bring it on board. It is of course pertinent to remember that conger eel is very good to eat; it gives beautiful white flesh and produces a relatively small amount of waste.

Play the fish until it is absolutely tired out; draw it towards your boat; and having cleared away any loose gear (buckets, oars, petrol cans and tackle boxes, etc), manoeuvre it so that your companion can put the gaff into its underside. Lift the fish on board and sever the spinal cord, just at the back of the head, as soon as possible. Use a very strong knife with a pointed blade.

Do not, under any circumstances, try to remove the hook from the conger's jaw with your bare hands and fingers; unclip the hook trace from the buckle, wait until the fish has been

28 A 65lb conger eel. This fish is capable of breaking a leg with a whack from its tail, and its jaw muscles have all the power necessary to drive its teeth through a rubber boot. Beware the conger, a ferocious marine eel

29 If you manage to land a conger, beware of those jaws—handle with the utmost care, but remember they make excellent eating. Their flesh is white and sweet and rivals turbot for 'meatiness'

gutted and *then* cut the hook free. *Never* try to bring a large conger into a small boat, and never try to deal with a conger of 15lb or more by yourself, unless you know exactly what you are doing and are on board a craft of suitable size.

Caution: spur dogfish

Spur dogfish are another hazardous species, and may well be found in rocky areas. They are a member of the shark family and have very unpleasant teeth, but this is not the primary reason for the danger. These fish derive their name from the vicious spines which are found immediately in front of both dorsal fins. These two spines are capable of penetrating the sole of a rubber boot, and the injuries they cause frequently turn septic. All injuries received as a result of handling these or any other fish should be treated immediately, and do not hesitate to seek specialist medical advice if you are at all worried.

Black bream

There is seldom any doubt over the hard snapping bite of a

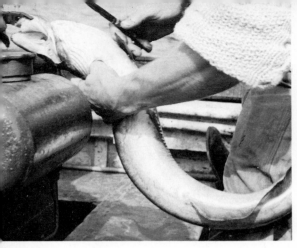

30 It usually takes two pairs of hands to recover the hook from a well hooked conger, a job which should not be attempted until the creature is dead. This is why it always pays to fish a hook on a detachable trace

3lb black bream. When these fish are in a taking mood, sport can be hectic. They can be caught on both ledger and paternoster tackle, size 6 or 8 hooks baited with lugworm, herring, squid or mussel.

Although these fish normally stay fairly close to the bottom during the height of the tide run, during slack water they move up somewhat, and then float tackle can be used. Neap tides can also give reasonable conditions for float fishing.

Black bream normally respond to a moving bait more readily than a static one. Use just enough weight to carry the hook and bait to the bottom, stop paying out line and let the

31 Spur dogfish. Good to eat but the possessor of dangerous needle-like spurs by the leading edge of the dorsal fin

tide's pull swing the bait like the upstroke of a pendulum. After a few moments, allow more line to run out slowly until the lead touches the sea bed once again. As you feel the lead strike, check the outflow of line. Repeat the technique again and again, so that the bait is fished downtide in a series of hops. It is possible, with care, to adopt this technique even when your equipment consists of nothing more elaborate than a handline.

Reduced to its most basic forms, a suitable arrangement for catching a few bream need employ no more than a few hundred feet of cod line, or something similar, a metal bolt or other weighty object, a few feet of 10lb BS nylon and a size 6 hook.

Tie the weight to one end of the line, and make a small loop in the line about 1ft up from the weight. Take 6ft of nylon monofilament line and tie a double overhand loop knot at one end and a hook to the other. Push the hook through the loop on the cod line, and then through the loop at the end of the nylon and pull tight. Bait the hook and start fishing.

Emergency lures

In an emergency, ignore all the accepted and recommended baits. Try a silver or gold milk-bottle top (squeeze the foil around the hook shank); a 3–4in-long thin strip of white cloth (possibly torn from a handkerchief), pieces of rubber or plastic cut to resemble a worm or small eel. Try anything you imagine might attract your quarry. You will be amazed at the vast array of items that will fool a fish.

Handle bream carefully

Take great care when handling bream; their dorsal fin has needle-sharp spines placed at the leading end, and these can open up a very unpleasant wound. When unhooking bream hold the fish from below, or, better still, cover the flattened dorsal fin with a cloth before holding firmly.

32 Black bream. Watch out for the needle-like spurs of its long dorsal fin. These fish are also covered with very coarse scales which must be removed before cooking, either by scraping or skinning the fish

Plaice, sole and dabs

A sea bed which is predominately mud, sand or shingle, or a reasonable mixture of all three, can produce an extremely wide variety of both flat and round fish.

Ledger tackle, as used for flounder fishing, is perfectly adequate for dabs, plaice and sole, but sole, being basically nocturnal creatures, are caught more easily at night. Hook sizes 4, 6 or 8 are suitable for all three species, and any of the marine worms make good bait. However, most of the largest plaice I have caught have fallen to either a small softback crab or a sand eel. Plaice will often snap at a moving bait more

33 A plaice, an easily identified fish which is frequently attracted by a moving bait, ragworm, lugworm and peeler crab are very acceptable to this species.

34 The rough skin of the dogfish, a member of the shark family, must be stripped before cooking. When first landed this fish will frequently wrap its sinuous body around hand and arm. Beware the rasp-like skin

readily than one just lying on the sea bed, but sole do not chase a bait in the same way.

Delicious dogfish

From the sporting standpoint, neither the greater nor lesser spotted dogfish are worthy of particular mention, but both are valuable as food. They usually take a ledgered fish bait, and it is quite incredible how a lesser spotted dogfish weighing possibly no more than about 2lb will devour a side of mackerel or herring baiting a size 4/0 or 6/0 hook meant for a thornback ray of 14lb or more.

As soon as a dogfish is brought on board, stun it with a heavy blow on the head, and unclip the trace and hook. Do not risk your fingers in the mouth of a dogfish, and beware of it wrapping its sinuous and very rough-skinned body around your hand and arm. The skin of a dogfish is quite capable of inflicting very severe grazing, often to the point of drawing blood.

When the fish has been stunned, open the gut with a sharp knife, clean it and *then* remove the hook and trace. Skinning a dogfish is not the easiest of chores, but the eating repays the effort. (See Chapter 8)

95

Beware of the sting ray

Both skate and ray are also difficult species to deal with when caught. Although there are quite a number of different rays in British waters—for example cuckoo, sandy, blonde, small-eyed, undulate, spotted, thornback and sting—the last two are the most dangerous. Of the two, the sting ray is certainly the most vicious: it has a whiplike tail armed with a long spike which can inflict a deep and quite horrifying wound. As the ray is brought on board, or indeed even when it is actually lying on the bottom boards of your boat, it is likely to whip its tail over and bury its serrated, daggerlike spike into your arm, hand or leg. Get to know the outline, shape and colouring of the sting ray and learn to identify it so that you will know exactly what you have caught, and will recognise it as soon as it is brought to the surface.

The sting ray is one of the few fish in British waters which has the capacity to inject venom into its victim's body. The spine on its tail has a groove lined with a venom-secreting tissue, and when this is injected into a human being it may even cause temporary paralysis, as well as the complications of septicemia. Immediately a sting ray is brought on board, pin the tail down with a broomhead or well booted foot, and then stun the ray with a heavy blow between the eyes. Sever the tail as close to the body as possible and dispose of it immediately.

The fish itself is not, in my opinion, worth eating; the flesh can be tough and it tastes strong. You can always offer the carcass to a professional fisherman to use in his pots or as bait on a trotline.

A word on weevers

While on the subject of unpleasant customers, mention must be made of the weever. There are in fact two weevers, the greater and lesser, but basically there is very little difference except in the maximum size to which they grow. The greater weever is mainly an inhabitant of the deeper offshore marks,

35 Danger poison! The greater weever, showing the dark, three-spined poison fin. Always seek medical advice if injured by one of these fish

and is therefore more likely to be taken by the boat angler; the lesser weever being a creature of shallow inshore waters where it tends to prefer a sandy, muddy bed. The lesser weever is quite often picked up in shrimpers' nets, so treat the small fish you find among the catch with great care.

Both greater and lesser weevers have a basically deep yellowy body which is overlayed with darker lines running at an oblique angle down both sides. They have venomous spines on the gill covers and first dorsal fin which are capable of inflicting very painful and even dangerous wounds.

The greater weever can attain a length of approximately 15–17in; the lesser weever may be half that size.

Fishing for skate and ray

The thornback ray has, as its name suggests, quite pronounced 'rosebush-like' thorns across its back. These protusions can open up a most unpleasant wound, so treat these fish with respect. Some would argue that they make the best eating of all the skates and rays, but this is a matter of opinion, and having eaten both undulate and blonde ray I would place several species on the same level.

Thornback ray are very widely distributed and are the species you are probably most likely to catch.

There is one feature common to all skates and rays—their

36 Still very much alive after a good fight: a thornback ray. Holding it like this is not a good idea—very rough on the hands

very powerful jaw muscles. A skate or ray of virtually any reasonable size can clamp its teeth on an unsuspecting finger and the vice-like grip will not be forgotten in a hurry. Skates and rays are very similar and from the fisherman's point of view there is hardly any difference at all. Both have a similar and well known outline shape, but there are some exceptions.

For example, the relatively rare species (in British water) such as the ox or horned ray and the electric ray are quite dis-

37 Safely gaffed, a thornback ray is swung aboard

38 Although 'flat' in appearance both skate and ray are 'round' fish. The wings are merely greatly thickened pectoral fins and it is these which make such good eating. However, the wings must be cut from the main body and skinned before cooking

tinctive. However, the basic similarity between the most commonly caught skates and rays is conveyed by the fact that, commercially, all these species are often referred to as 'roker'.

Skates and rays are normally caught on ledger tackle, using a nylon-covered steel trace of some 30 or 40lb BS, and a size 4/0 or 6/0 hook baited with a fillet of herring or mackerel. I favour using a trace some 3ft long and, for preference, swivelled half way.

It is often possible to identify a ray as soon as it begins mouthing the bait. It will frequently flop onto the baited hook so that you will feel a sudden heaviness. As its jaws begin grinding at the bait, the sensation is transmitted along the line and you can feel it. This is difficult to describe, but if you imagine what is happening to your baited hook, you may possibly be able to translate this into feeling.

Never be in a hurry when fishing for skate and ray; give the fish plenty of time to inspect and accept the bait. You will know when it is time to strike as the fish will begin to move away and draw line from the reel. As the run develops, strike hard and drive the hook home. It is seldom that you will get any violent reaction from these fish. Frequently they will do no more than attempt to sulk on the sea bed, and a really big

39 In the record class. Big skate have been caught on small reels and light tackle that seem impossibly inadequate—this heavyweight tipped the scales at 100lb—but you must remember the habits of the fish, know the limitations of your tackle, and have a lot of endurance and common sense

fish can take quite an amount of moving. However, once it is off the ground, and if there is a fairly strong tide running, a skate or ray can spread its 'wings' and take advantage of the current. When this happens it can be like trying to control a large kite in a gale of wind, and the result can be a relatively spirited battle.

Eventually it will tire and you will be able to bring it alongside. It is at this point that it becomes useful to be able to identify the more dangerous species. Gaff or net skates and rays as you would any other fish; bring the fish to the gaff or net, never chase the fish. Generally speaking they are easier to gaff, as, if the fish is of any size, you will be hard put to find a net large enough to cope with its wing span and tail. Drive the gaff hook into its underside and swing the fish on board.

Their bodies have a liberal coating of slime, and therefore they should always be placed straight into a fish tray. They are usually relatively docile once laid flat; a quick thrust downwards between the eyes with a pointed strong bladed knife and the fish will be dead, and the creature is then ready for 'winging'. (See Chapter 8.)

Turbot and brill

When considering the cost of fish these days, it may sound

little short of ridiculous to suggest cutting up a mackerel to use as bait. But given luck and the right circumstances it is possible to turn one lonely mackerel lying in a fish tray into multi-pound turbot or brill. Apart from the sand eels, few other baits are more likely to lure one or other of these highly prized species.

Sand, gravel or mud banks are the favoured environment of turbot and brill, and they can be caught in depths ranging from 2—3 fathoms to 50—60 fathoms. However, scientific investigation indicates that most commercially caught turbot is taken from marks ranging in depths from around 20—50 fathoms.

Both turbot and brill are basically predatory fish, with sand eel and the fry of many other species forming a large part of their diet. This being so it is only natural that they would be attracted to a bait consisting of these creatures, or a strip of fresh fish cut from a mackerel or herring.

All the turbot that I have caught have been taken while fishing a moving bait. In other words, either the boat has been drifting over suitable ground, or I have been casting and then slowly recovering the bait, or fishing in such a way that the bait was being carried over the sea bed by the tide. No doubt many fishermen have caught both turbot and brill on a static bait, but in my opinion one which is moving will be more likely to catch them.

Fig 16 Turbot and brill. Brill and turbot are two very similar species. Turbot tend to be more diamond-shaped than brill and also have bony tubercles on the upper, or eyed, side. Brill are more rounded and do not have tubercles on either side

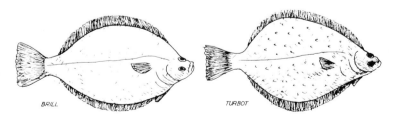

BRILL   TURBOT

40 Landing a turbot, but not a method to be recommended. Many a tasty dinner has been lost through lack of net or gaff. These fish are often caught on a strip of freshly caught mackerel, and they frequently are more interested in a moving bait, one drawn slowly over the sea bed

When fishing specifically for turbot in an area where they are known to be, use a size 3/0 or 4/0 hook, possibly a Sea-master or Model Perfect forged-steel hook tied to a 25lb BS trace. Although these fish have sharp teeth, it is not necessary to use a steel trace. However, if turbot are only one of a number of species known to frequent the mark you are fishing, then you may be well advised to use a nylon-covered steel trace. This will give added security should you hook a large thornback or similar fish.

Brill, although very similar to turbot in virtually every respect, are a smaller species. At the time of writing the British record for a rod-caught turbot stands at just over 31lb; the brill record is approximately half—16lb. So use similar tactics as for turbot but use a smaller hook.

Garfish and John Dory

The garfish and John Dory look quite odd, but both are good to eat. The garfish is an eel-like fish with a long pointed

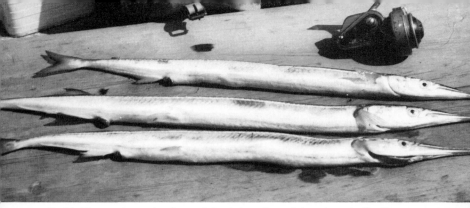

41 Garfish. These marine acrobats frequently break the surface and almost 'cartwheel' as if thoroughly enjoying life. However, they are great hunters who harry shoals of smaller fish and can be caught on spinners, feathers and other moving lures

snout. It has many local names including 'sea pike', 'guard fish', 'long nose' and 'greenbone', but it is this last name, greenbone, which gives a clue to one of its peculiarities.

When these fish are cleaned and cooked, and in my opinion they are delicious, the bones are green. This fact is disliked by some, but for all that the flesh is still excellent and is not affected at all by the coloured bones.

Garfish are widely distributed, and frequently take a spinner or feather meant to lure a bass or mackerel.

The John Dory contrasts strongly with the fast moving and acrobatic garfish. It is just about the most odd-looking of all the fish which are relatively common in our waters. Its body is oval and compressed, rather like a plaice, but it swims in an upright position, not on its side as flatfish do.

It has two dorsal fins, the leading one having long filaments trailing from it; the pelvic fins are similarly decorated. Its mouth, when opened, extends into a funnel-like protrusion, and on either side of its body it sports a dark patch. Along the base of both the anal and dorsal fins there is a row of spines, and it carries similar armament along the belly from vent to throat. All in all, it is a peculiar-looking fish. However, the flesh is excellent; there are few fish which give better. The fillets are firm, white and sweet to the taste.

John Dory are frequently caught on paternoster or ledger tackle, but as they tend to be solitary fish which 'bumble around' they are usually hooked by accident rather than design.

Eels

Eels can live in both salt and fresh water, and the eel caught in harbour or estuary is kin to the one hooked many miles from the sea, maybe in a Midlands canal or brickyard pit.

The eel's cycle is fascinating, beginning deep in the Atlantic, somewhere south and east of Bermuda, and continuing with a journey of two years or more across the ocean to our shores. Eventually, maybe eight or nine years later, the eels begin the return journey. They leave their fenland drains, canals, rivers, ponds and lakes, and start a seaward migration which ends in spawning and death in the area where their story began.

No matter where they are caught, in freshwater or salt, eels make excellent eating. In fact, many extensive and extremely valuable eel fisheries are operated commercially. In a number of countries, eel flesh, particularly when smoked, commands a price equal to and often greater than that asked for smoked salmon or trout. When ledger fishing for plaice, flounder or bass, do not despise the eels you frequently catch; they represent highly nutricious and valuable food.

A final word

These are the species which form the bulk of the catches made by fishermen in British waters, with emphasis on those species which make good eating. There is, I feel, one aspect which must not be overlooked. Because sea fish are freely available to anyone, remember that freedom brings responsibility if you wish to take advantage of this fact.

The right to fish is not a licence to pillage and destroy. Take that which is fair and reasonable and no more; stick to the rules, and think of others. The sea is not limitless in its resources; only the criminally stupid eat the seed corn.

7 In Praise of Shellfish

As a source of food from the sea, shellfish come a close second to the true fish. For commercial and trading purposes the term 'shellfish' also includes members of the crab and lobster family, creatures which, in the true sense, are crustaceans. This chapter deals exclusively with shellfish both as food and bait, crustaceans being covered separately but in a similar manner in Chapter 2.

Shellfish, for example oysters, mussels, scallops, whelks, winkles and the like, are molluscs; and Britain, having a shellfish industry which is of comparatively small importance, lags behind many other maritime countries. Nevertheless, many shellfish provide an excellent and welcome source of food, as well as being useful for bait.

Mussels

After the oyster the common mussel is the most important molluscan shellfish used as food in Europe, and is so common that it hardly needs description—most people must be familiar with its shape and dark-blue shell.

It is abundant in sheltered parts of the coast, particularly in estuaries, and is generally to be found clinging, by means of its fibrous 'foot', to piles, rocks and stones on the sea bed. Mussels form colonies or beds which are extremely dense and generally only exposed at periods of very low tide.

Mussels can be kept alive for a considerable period, providing they are dipped in sea water at regular intervals, or kept in a perforated box or basket suspended over the side of a boat.

Cockles

The edible cockle is probably familiar to most people who

have some association with the sea or seashore. A good aver-age-sized cockle is about 1in long and has a rounded shell covered with small protuberances which enable it to grip the sand in which it lives. The colour of the shell may vary from almost pure white to a faint shade of orange.

The cockle is usually found between tide marks, generally where there is a stretch of sand sheltered from currents and from the full force of the sea. It normally lies just beneath the sand so that one end of the shell is just flush with the surface, yet it is able to move about in the sand or on the surface by using a 'foot' which is surprisingly muscular.

Like all bivalve molluscs, cockles live on small organisms in the sea water and not on substances which may be in the sand.

Cockles are good to eat, and can generally be collected by drawing a small garden rake or metal hook through the sand. They can also be taken from the mud in estuaries, but they must be carefully cleaned and they also tend to be slightly stronger flavoured than mussels.

Whelks

The whelk lives in a spiral shell, unlike the mussels and cockles which have hinged shells. It has a tough, leathery sec-tion of skin which can be drawn over the entrance to the shell to protect it from its enemies.

It can move along the sea bed rather like a snail and gener-ally lives on fish, other shellfish and waste matter.

Scallops

With its round markings and radiating grooves, the scallop is possibly the most attractive of all shells, and one which has been used for ornamentation and design for many hundreds of years. Scallops have attractive interiors with red, white, and orange hues. They are expensive to buy, and not easily collected by the average person except on the western coast of Scotland.

Oysters

The oyster is largely a shallow-water shellfish with a decided preference for estuaries. Most oyster fisheries are seeded, and therefore under strict control. Generally they are far too expensive and rare to use for bait, but they are very attractive to bass and other fish.

Winkles

These are extremely small and are found attached to rocks, piles and, in some areas, on shingle banks. They are similar in shape to whelks but without the ribbing on the shell, and are usually grey, black or dark brown.

Winkles are prolific, and a good quantity can be collected in a short while.

Gathering shellfish

Mussels, cockles, whelks, winkles, scallops and oysters form the main supply of shellfish for human consumption, and whether for bait or for eating they are gathered in a similar fashion. Rock-clinging limpets can also be eaten but they are extremely tough and not very palatable.

It used to be said that shellfish should only be eaten when there was an 'R' in the month, but this was a custom carried on from the days before refrigeration and cold stores. It was to avoid the possibility of stale shellfish being sold during the hot summer months, and the consequential risk of infection and food poisoning.

With the advent of improved storage facilities, shellfish can now be obtained generally all the year round, but 'close' seasons are imposed by some local fisheries and districts, and anyone proposing to gather shellfish would be wise to make the necessary enquiries to avoid embarrassment and possibly a fine.

Shellfish provide a valuable source of food as they store great quantities of glycogen, or animal starch, as well as fat and protein: and they are a complete food in themselves.

Unfortunately there is one great drawback to the consumption of shellfish, and that is the risk of bacterial infection. Rigorous regulations forbid the sale of polluted shellfish but the risk of disease has been an important (and in the past not unjustified) reason for the undoubted prejudice against the use of shellfish for food.

Where shellfish are collected, both in esturial waters and from the open foreshore, great care should be taken to enquire whether they are generally collected by other persons and offered for sale, or whether there are any regulations forbidding their use as food. Obviously if this is the case they should not be used.

One could easily be led to believe that shellfish collected along the foreshore of an open beach would be clean and free from infection, but this may not be the case. The far too common practice of pumping partially treated sewage out to sea has polluted many inshore shellfish beds, as all too often the polluting agents find their way back onto the beaches.

Where cockles and mussels are suitable for human consumption, they should, before cooking, be carefully scrubbed externally to remove any weed growth, mud or other impurity, then placed in a polythene bucket of strong brine solution or covered with neat salt to allow them to 'spit', whereby they remove all the waste products of the stomach and also any sand which may have accumulated internally.

It is absolutely essential to clean the fish in this manner, otherwise they are almost totally inedible.

There are a considerable number of ways of cooking shellfish, from simply boiling them in salted water (as for winkles) to the preparation of *moules marinière*. Recipes for cooking shellfish can be found in any good quality cookery book.

8 Cleaning and Cooking Your Catch

Killing, gutting and cleaning

It is seldom necessary to kill your catch, as in the vast majority of cases a fish will suffocate very quickly when taken from the water. There are a few exceptions to this rule; the dogfish is possibly the best example of a fish which will survive for some time out of water. At the other end of the scale there is the mackerel, which ceases all movement within seconds.

When it is necessary to kill a fish, do it quickly, severing its spinal cord with a knife. Use a knife with a strong, pointed blade, which will also serve for gutting and cutting large fish into manageable portions. For skinning and filleting, a sharp-pointed knife with a thin flexible blade is usually handier.

A cutting board is also important, a square of beechwood is ideal, though not cheap to buy new. Sometimes a suitable board can be found in a second-hand furniture store. The main point to remember is that unless a cutting board is used, it is inevitable that someone will damage a varnished seat or gunwale.

You also need a good pair of pliers, rags, an oilstone or other sharpener for your knife, one or two buckets and a fish tray. It really is most unhygienic to leave fish that is going to be eaten lying around either on the deck or in an old and dirty box.

Fish that are destined for the table should be gutted and cleaned as soon as possible, and most fish can be gutted quickly and easily. Insert the knife point into the vent and cut toward the head; this lays open the stomach cavity which is then cleaned out. Once this has been done the fish can be left for several hours. However, do not leave it where the wind and sun can dry both scales and skin; this is particularly im-

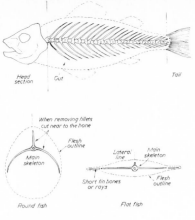

Fig 17 The skeletons of round and flatfish

portant if the catch is destined for the deep freeze. Any deterioration in quality should be avoided when flesh is to be kept frozen for a period.

Cleaning and filleting

A fish is cooked either whole or in pieces. If whole, it may or may not be left complete with head, but the scales and spurs must always be removed. Once the scales become dry they are more difficult to remove, and when scraped from the skin they will tend to fly in all directions. To avoid unnecessary mess, lay the fish under water and then scrape from tail to head. Trim fins and spurs with either a sharp knife or scissors.

If the fish is to be cooked complete with head, make sure that the mouth is thoroughly cleaned, and also remove the gill filaments.

A fish must be fairly large before it is worth slicing into cutlets. Even with a round fish, such as cod or bass, weighing about 10lb or more, there would not be more than two or three reasonable cutlets before the reduced body size made it necessary to fillet.

When removing the head before cutting either the first cutlet or fillet, do not waste prime flesh by slicing straight down from back to belly. Follow the cutting lines on the diagrams. Do not be in a hurry, cut carefully and angle the knife

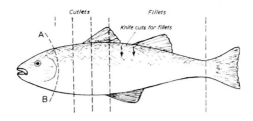

Fig 18 Cutlets and fillets. Trim fins and remove the head by cutting from A to B. Cut three or more cutlets, depending on the size of the fish. Remove fillets from the rear section. Slice downwards, from positions on either side of the trimmed fins, following the shape of the skeleton

blade slightly towards the bone. This will ensure the maximum amount of flesh is removed.

Skinning dogfish

After gutting the fish remove each of its fins, cutting flush with the body. Always cut from the tail towards the head. Using just the knife tip, score a line from head to tail right down the centre of the back, and make another score mark on the underside, continuing from the vent to tail. These score marks are meant to do no more than penetrate the skin. Do not remove the head.

Finally, use your knife to make another score mark around what could be termed its neck. You can now lift a corner of skin, high up on the body on either side, where the lateral score mark along the back joins the cut around its neck. Place a piece of rag around the head, hold the head tight, and using the pliers strip the skin right down one half of the body. Repeat the process on the other half, chop off the tail and head, and you are left with several pounds of delicious flesh.

Skate and ray

When you catch a skate or ray, remember that these are round fish which have developed in such a way that their pectoral fins have become greatly enlarged. It is these pectoral fins or 'wings' which you must now remove, as they are

III

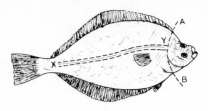

Fig 19 To fillet a typical flatfish, eg flounder, plaice etc, remove head and gut by cutting along the dotted line A–B. Cut down to the bone along line X–Y, and then slice outwards, following the layout of the skeleton. Repeat, and remove all four fillets

the sections which produce the edible meat. The diagram shows the approximate positioning of the fish's main body and by following the cutting line both pectoral fins can be removed and be prepared for cooking.

Once the wings are removed they must be skinned. This is the most difficult part of the whole operation, and unless done carefully can result in grazed fingers. Start by laying the wings on a cutting board, thick edge toward you. Hold firmly, using a piece of clean rag to protect hand and fingers, and with a very sharp but thin-bladed knife, begin separating skin from flesh.

As soon as a flap large enough to hold has been lifted turn the wing around and, holding the inner edge of the wing with one hand, strip the skin either by hand or with a pair of pliers. Treat both the upper and lower side the same way.

Fig 20 Cutting the wings from a thornback ray. When the 'wings' are removed, lay the fish on a spiked board and remove the skin, both upper and lower sides, with a sharp, thin-bladed knife and pliers (see text p114)

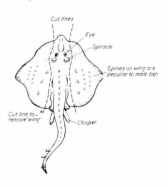

If the wing is large and difficult to skin you may well find a spiked board useful. I keep a square of beechwood specifically for this purpose. Drive a nail or two through the board, and use the protruding point to anchor the wing.

Lay the wings on the board, and begin as before by lifting a flap. Once a fair-sized flap of skin has been cleared, turn the board around, and once again try to strip the skin manually. If this is not possible, continue with the knife blade, but, as you cut, angle the blade upwards towards the underside of the skin. This will enable you to make a relatively clean and complete removal.

Perform this task slowly and methodically, remembering all the while that what you are cutting is not only very good to eat, but also as valuable as pork or lamb.

Skinning other fish

Apart from the dogfish, skate and ray, there are several other fish which are also more easily dealt with if skinned. Bass, bream and red mullet are covered with large coarse scales which should be removed before cooking. If these fish are destined to be cooked on the bone, then one need do no more than gut, trim the fins and generally clean and scrape the body to remove the scales, and then cut off the head. But fil-

Fig 21 Skinning a bass. Cut through (not deeply) the skin covering both sides, following the dotted line. When the score line is complete, lift the flap of skin at point A. Grip the head with hand protected by a clean cloth, grasp the flap of skin with pliers and pull towards the tail. If done firmly and correctly, the skin will come away very easily. Cut a fillet from each side

leting is made a lot easier if both skin and scales are removed together. This is a simple operation, just as long as the score marks are clean and not too deep. Ideally the cut line should just penetrate the skin. Lift a corner of skin, grasp the fish's head in one hand and strip the skin down towards the tail with the other.

Recipes

Bass

Bass can be sliced into cutlets or filleted, and then cooked in a variety of ways ranging from grilling to deep frying in batter. However, bass have a slightly dry flesh, and are delicious when stuffed and baked in the oven.

Gut and thoroughly clean the fish, remove the scales but not the skin or head.

For stuffing, lightly fry a couple of rashers of streaky bacon, cut them into strips and mix them in a bowl with chopped hard-boiled egg, prawns or shrimps, mushrooms and a small amount of breadcrumbs (these ingredients can be measured according to taste). Finally, add a few drops of fresh lemon juice and a pinch of basil.

Force the stuffing into the stomach cavity, lay a few rashers of streaky bacon along both sides of the fish, wrap it in foil and bake in a medium oven for approximately 30–40 minutes per pound (including weight of stuffing).

When the fish is cooked, allow it to cool slowly in its juices. Do not remove the foil until the fish has cooled slowly and completely.

Lay the fish on a serving dish, chill slightly in the refrigerator, then decorate it with olives, cucumber, lettuce, and lemon etc. Served cold with a salad, it is magnificent.

Bream

These fish have a covering of large and extremely coarse scales. Once these are removed the fish can be cooked whole on the bone (either grilled or fried). Many prefer to skin, fillet, and then bake the fillets in the oven in a covered dish.

The fillets can be grilled, and just before serving, dusted with grated parmesan cheese, returned under the heat, browned and then served.

However, despite the obvious advantages of these relatively simple ways of cooking bream, this quite ordinary fish can be transformed by being slightly more adventurous.

Take approximately 2lb of bream fillets and lay them in a baking dish, season, and add the juice of half a lemon. Almost cover with thick cream (about $\frac{1}{2}$pt), and sprinkle with 2–3oz of grated parmesan cheese. Dot the fish with several pieces of butter, and bake it in a moderate oven (approximately 370 degrees F), for about 20–25 minutes. Serve it hot with your favourite mixed vegetables.

Coalfish (coley or saithe)

An easily cleaned and prepared species; no need to skin.

These fish can be fairly sizeable, so why not take advantage of an interesting recipe, one which is based on a really thick cutlet, something weighing 2lb or more.

Lay the cutlet, belly down, in a large but shallow casserole. Salt and pepper the fish and rub it into the skin. Cut $\frac{1}{4}$lb of streaky bacon rashers into strips and add $\frac{1}{2}$lb of button mushrooms. Place both bacon and mushrooms in a dish and around the cutlet. Smear the fish liberally with butter and bake it in a moderate oven for about 50 minutes.

This recipe can be varied considerably. For example, instead of coalfish, either cod or pollack can be used, or even ling. Onions and/or tomatoes can be used instead of, or as well as, mushrooms. Some may even fancy the addition of an amount of curry powder, this being sprinkled over the fish before baking. This dish can be served hot with potatoes, or cold with salad.

Cod

Crispy fried with chips may be the traditional way of serving cod, but like the previously mentioned species, cod is easy to prepare, so why not be adventurous? Grilled cod cutlets with mushrooms and almonds are easy to prepare, making an extremely quick meal which needs the minimum of fuss.

Lay the cutlets down in a grill pan in which an amount of butter has been melted. Turn the cutlets once so that both sides are greased, sprinkle lightly with salt, pepper and parmesan cheese and cook under moderate heat until golden and tender. Turn the cutlets over and repeat the process.

While the cutlets are grilling, fry some almonds in butter (1oz to each cutlet) with an equal weight of mushrooms.

When the fish is cooked, lay it on a serving dish, surround it with mushrooms and nuts, garnish with parsley and serve.

Other fish besides cod can be used in the recipe: turbot, brill, haddock and similar white fish.

Conger

Once the eel has been gutted, cleaned and its head removed, an extremely nutricious and high quality white flesh is left.

Some favour skinning, but this I do not consider necessary. Slice thick cutlets from the body starting immediately behind the head: this can be continued for approximately two-thirds of the body length, until it becomes too thin and bony to worry about.

These cutlets can be either steamed or boiled in water salted to taste; when cooked, serve with creamed potatoes and parsley sauce.

Conger steaks can also be baked in foil or cooked in other ways already described.

One old Cornish recipe describes the making of conger pie. Choose several good thick cutlets and coat them with seasoned flour. Lay the conger into a deep, well greased casserole dish, add several knobs of butter and parsley to taste. Add milk and cook slowly in a moderate oven until about half cooked. Add some fresh cream, top with a shortcrust pastry lid, and finish in a hot oven.

Chopped chives or mushrooms can be added if desired.

Dogfish

From the culinary standpoint these are probably the most underrated fish in the sea, but, as they form quite a sizeable proportion of the sea fisherman's general catch, it is important to make the best of them. Dogfish have a most unfortunate name, and no doubt this is why they are often described by the trade as 'Dutch eel', 'huss' or even 'rock salmon'. However, a dogfish is a dogfish, and no amount of name-changing will alter the fact that it is an easily cooked and tasty fish.

It can be cooked in many ways, ranging from the traditional 'deep fried in batter' to the more exotic 'curried dogfish'.

The list of ingredients is quite impressive, starting with cooking oil and ending with a couple of pounds of fish which has been cleaned, skinned and cut into portions. Filling in between oil and fish there are items such as a large apple and an onion of equal size, one carrot and two or three tomatoes. A tablespoonful of flour, curry powder to taste, 1–2oz of sultanas and a tablespoonful of dessicated coconut, the juice of one fresh lemon and about half a pint of stock will also be needed.

Chop the vegetables and cook them in oil. When soft add the sultanas and continue cooking slowly until the vegetables colour, add the curry powder and continue cooking for another 5–7 minutes.

Make a sauce with flour and stock, heat it slowly and then add to the curried vegetables. Continue cooking the sauce slowly until it thickens, pour half into a casserole dish, arrange the fish pieces and pour the remaining sauce over the fish. Bake it slowly for about 40–50 minutes. When cooked, add coconut and lemon juice to taste.

This dish can be served with rice, or if you prefer, creamed or boiled potatoes.

Many other recipes exist for cooking dogfish; they vary from poaching in salted water flavoured with garlic, to baking with cream and parmesan cheese in a casserole.

Dogfish have no small or sharp bones to worry about, and are therefore often a children's favourite.

Eels

Eels are another much underrated fish. The flesh is firm, white and sweet, and they can be cooked in a number of ways.

Clean and gut, score around the 'collar', wrap the head in rag and hold tightly and strip the skin with a pair of pliers. Eels skin quite easily. Cut the body into chunks, dust with seasoned flour and fry in butter.

For *jellied eels*, thoroughly clean and remove the head; trim the fins and cut the body into chunks. (Do not skin).

Once again clean and then lay the pieces of eel in a pan, cover with fresh water and bring this slowly to the boil. Rinse the eel under running cold water and then replace it in the pan; once again cover with fresh water, add salt to taste, bring it slowly to the boil and simmer for about 20 minutes.

When cooked, pour both fish and liquid into a bowl and leave it in the refrigerator to set. Gelatine is not necessary unless you want a really thick jelly.

This basic recipe can be varied in a number of ways. For example, the eel flesh can be cooked with parsley, onion, vinegar and bay leaf; when cooked, add the whisked white of a couple of eggs, salt and pepper. If desired, add 1–2oz of leaf gelatine, bring to the boil once again and then pour into a bowl and allow to set.

Flounder

Flounders are easy to deal with: just remove the head and gut. They can be smeared with butter, sprinkled with sea-food spices and then grilled on the bone.

The fillets are excellent deep-fried in batter, or cooked on a buttered plate placed on top of a saucepan of simmering water. This latter method is both quick and simple, and the fillets can be made more enticing by adding a spoonful of cream, chopped chives or even a light sprinkling of dry mustard powder.

Fillets cut from a sizeable flounder (or indeed from any flatfish) can be used to create a particularly interesting dish of *rolled fillets with lemon sauce*.

Roll each fillet, skin side out, and secure with a cocktail stick. Lay the fillets in a deep saucepan, cover them with cold court bouillon and heat this slowly. Simmer it until the fish is cooked—this should be in about 10–12 minutes.

Prepare the lemon sauce while the fillets are cooking. Lay the fillets, when cooked, in a casserole dish, remove the sticks and keep the fish warm until the sauce is ready. Pour sauce over the fillets, and then decorate them with shrimps, parsley and thin slices of lemon.

Flounder fillets are delicious when dipped in beaten egg, covered in breadcrumbs and fried in butter.

Garfish

Clean, gut and scrape the scales, or skin the fish; cut it into sections, coat it with seasoned flour and fry it in butter. Ignore the green bones!

Haddock

A fish which gives excellent firm white flesh which can be cooked in a number of ways. Prepare the fish and scrape the skin, fillet and fry in any of the previously suggested ways, or roll and present with lemon or cheese sauce.

Grill on the bone—bake in foil with mushrooms—or why not try making a *fish chowder*. This way nothing is wasted.

Clean and skin the fish (about 2lb) removing gill filaments and eyeballs; fillet, and cut the fillets into half-inch squares.

Place all oddments (head, bones and tail) into a saucepan with 1pt water, bring this to the boil and simmer for half an hour. While this is slowly cooking, dice 2–3oz of salt pork and fry them until the fat is golden brown; add chopped onion; cover and cook this slowly for a further 10 minutes.

Transfer the pork and onion to a saucepan, add ½pt of water, and 1lb of diced potato. Bring this to the boil and simmer for 5–7 minutes. Add the stock from the bones, the cubes of fish, a knob of butter and ½pt of scalded milk. Simmer for about 10 minutes, adding salt and pepper to taste. Serve with a dash of cream.

Mackerel

An easy fish to both clean and cook. Remove the head, open the gut and thoroughly clean, and it is then ready to be either split open or grilled whole. If mackerel are to be cooked whole, score the sides, grease the grill and brush with melted butter, then grill until the skin turns brown. Serve with a knob of butter, parsley and slices of lemon.

Mackerel split for cooking should be grilled flesh side first, and can be sprinkled with a small amount of finely chopped shallot or onion.

Soused mackerel are excellent with salad. Clean the fish and remove head and fins. Lay it head to tail in a large flat casserole, and cover with a half-and-half mixture of pure malt vinegar and water. Add pickling spices to your own taste, plus a bay leaf and at least one large sliced onion.

Cook this slowly for 2 hours or more; exact timing depends upon the size of the fish. Allow to cool slowly, and let it stand at least 24 hours in a cool larder. Serve cold with chilled, dry white wine and salad.

Never use stale mackerel, they are a poor apology for fresh.

Smoked mackerel are a speciality of Cornwall and Devon, and many consider them superior to any other smoked fish.

Plaice

A well known fish which is simple to prepare and can be cooked in a variety of ways.

Filleted and cooked as previously suggested for flounders, grilled or fried on the bone, steamed or baked in the oven with cheese.

However, for one particular recipe the requirements are: one plaice per person, eggs, mushrooms, breadcrumbs, shrimps and a few rashers of streaky or boiled collar bacon.

Clean each fish, gut and remove the head, and lay the fish on a cutting board, spots uppermost. Place the point of a filleting knife onto the line running down the centre of its back, and slicing down to the bone and then outwards, cut a 'pocket' into the fillet on each side of the centre line.

Make sure that the knife cuts do not go out of the side of the fish. To be successful the 'pockets' must be secure.

Hard boil one egg per fish, and fry strips of bacon with chopped mushroom. When cooked, add chopped hard-boiled egg, shrimps and breadcrumbs, plus seasoning to taste.

Lay the fish in a buttered grill pan and cook the underside first; turn, stuff the pockets with the egg, bacon and shrimp mixture, brush with melted butter and grill. Serve with slices of lemon, grilled tomato and chips.

Skate and ray

The skinned wings of both skate and ray can be fried or grilled. However, cooked slowly in the oven with mushrooms, parsley and onions, they are excellent.

Cut the wings into 2in slices (cut following the line of bone) and lay in a suitable, buttered, fireproof dish. Both surround and cover the fish with sliced mushroom, onion and parsley with salt and black pepper to taste. Cover and cook in a medium oven for about one hour.

Make a basic white sauce with flour, butter and the liquid from the fish. Pour the sauce over the fish, sprinkle it with breadcrumbs and brown under the grill. A slight variation can be made by adding a small amount of grated parmesan cheese to the breadcrumbs.

Sole

Sole can be cooked in any one of a vast number of ways, ranging from the exotic fillets of *sole bonne femme* to the more mundane fried sole and chips. Whichever you choose, *remember that sole must be skinned.*

Wash and dry the fish, remove the fins and lay the fish down on a cutting board, tail towards you. Score the skin just above the tail, and after lifting the first inch carefully, jerk the skin quickly and firmly towards the head; it should strip quite easily.

When dealing with sole, or indeed any other species, it sometimes helps to dip your fingers into salt; this will improve your grip.

Sole are the only flatfish that are skinned on the bone. If it is thought necessary to skin flounders, dabs or plaice, remove the fillets first, and then lay the fillet down and cut from tail towards head, angling the knife downwards while cutting.

Turbot

Both turbot and brill are highly prized flatfish, and as such can be treated identically. As with sole there are many exotic recipes, but one of the nicest is baked turbot with shrimp or prawn sauce.

Slice the fish into pieces of a suitable size and lay in a buttered, fireproof dish. Add seasoning to taste, plus an amount of fresh lemon juice. Cover with fresh single cream, and bake slowly in a moderate oven. If practical, stand the dish containing the fish in a larger dish of water.

Baste often while the turbot is cooking, and also make a shrimp or prawn sauce, which is poured over the portions of fish when served.

This basic recipe can be altered to suit individual taste. For example, mushrooms, prawns or even lobster can be added while cooking, and turbot baked and served with a cheese sauce is also delicious.

Crab, crawfish and lobster

The cooking of these delicious crustaceans tends to be invested with an amount of mystique. However, given a large enough pan and a small amount of know-how, the average fisherman can manage very satisfactorily.

Lay the live crab into a pan of cold water, and bring slowly to the boil. Simmer for about 20 minutes and cool naturally.

All the meat within the claws is edible. The coral or red meat inside is just as delicious as the other flesh, but the rather rubbery 'fingerlike' section should be discarded. To get to the interior of the crab, lift the shell from the rear. The shell can be cleaned and dried and the flesh arranged in it. Season with a few drops of lemon juice, vinegar, salt and pepper etc, and serve with salad.

The crawfish (and do not confuse this animal with the fresh-water crayfish) is really no more than a spiny, clawless lobster. It is cooked in the same way as lobster and the meat is almost indistinguishable.

A lobster can be boiled in either fresh water or court bouillon. Bring the liquid to the boil and put in the live lobster head first. It is important to remember that the lobster should not be put into the water tail first with its underside towards you. If it is placed in the water incorrectly its tail can flip boiling water into your face.

When the lobster is cooked it will be a bright red. This normally takes about 20 minutes, possibly a little longer if it is a really big one. Allow the lobster to cool in the liquid, and then pick the white meat from the small claws, crack the large claws and scrape all the white flesh from inside.

Split the tail with a sharp knife, cut downwards and slightly to one side. This will disclose the intestinal cord. Remove this cord and all the flesh that remains here is edible.

Open the main body and use the bright red coral and the green liver—it is all extremely good to eat. Discard the spongy tissue lying between shell and meat, and also the stomach which lays high up in the top of the head.

Appendix

Some basic angling terms

action—descriptive of the flexing of a rod in casting or playing a fish.

blank—section of rod material to which rings and handle have still to be fitted. If you wanted to build your own rod, you might ask for two cane or glassfibre blanks.

cast—the action of throwing line or tackle; *also* the leader which carries the baited hook from the main line.

courge—a wickerwork container for keeping bait alive by constantly irrigating it with fresh seawater.

flatties—familiar word for flatfish, embracing dabs, flounders, sole and plaice.

gaff—large barbless hook, mounted on a handle, used for landing heavy fish.

gape—space between the shank and the point of a hook.

ledger or leger—the method of fishing on the bottom with weights, either stationary or moving with the tide. The bite is indicated by the movement of the rod tip.

mark—the area over which a sea angler fishes.

paternoster—a wire boom extension, fitted to the main line, for deploying a cast and hook (can have single or multiple booms).

penner—a perforated box for keeping bait alive in the same way as the courge.

run—a long length of line stripped from the reel by a fish after taking a bait.

snag—any obstacle in which a hook or tackle may be caught, or in which a fish may entangle itself or use to break the line.

snood—the cast and hook attached to a trotline.

strike—the action of the rod which sets the hook into a fish after the bait is taken (usually an upward sweeping action).

trotline—a stout length of line to which snoods are attached, fastened to the sea bed at low tide or lowered from a boat and subsequently recovered.

Further Reading

Books

Barrett, J. H. & Yonge, C. M., *Pocket Guide to the Seashore* (Collins, 1958)

Forbes, David Carl, *Successful Sea Angling* (David & Charles)

Jenkins, Travis, *The Fishes of the British Isles* (Frederick Warne, 1925)

Kennedy, Michael, *The Sea Angler's Fishes* (Hutchinson, 1954)

Lythgoe, John & Gillian, *Fishes of the Seas* (Blandford Press, 1971)

Street, P., *Between the Tides* (University of London Press, 1963)

Wilson, D. P., *Life of the Shore and Shallow Sea* (Ivor Nicholson & Watson, 1935)

Wrangles, Alan (ed), *Complete Guide to Sea Angling* (David & Charles, 1973)

Periodicals

Angling
Fisherman
Sea Angler

Acknowledgements

All photographs used are by permission of William J. Howes excepting Plate 5, which is by permission of the Northern Ireland Tourist Board, and Plate 9 which belongs to the author.

Index

David & Charles have a book on it

The Complete Guide to Sea Angling Edited by Alan Wrangles. This latest, revised edition of one of the most popular and comprehensive guides to sea angling yet published incorporates the most recent discoveries of the scientists and describes how they are being successfully applied in practice by some of the greatest masters of the angling art. Every facet of the sport is covered from the choice of tackle, identification of species and where to fish, to the techniques of beach casting, fishing from rocks and piers, and the art of boat handling. Forty-one species of fish and their habits are described and the work is illustrated by 65 photographs and 175 brilliant drawings by David Carl Forbes.

Guide to Shore and Harbour Fishing by F. H. Burgess. Shore and harbour fishing, whether from a pier or jetty, a small boat in an estuary or casting from a sandy beach, calls for techniques and tackle differing in many ways from deep-sea angling. This book, intended primarily for newcomers to the sport, explains the various methods to be employed under a variety of conditions, gives practical advice on the choice of equipment, and includes detailed drawings to facilitate identification of some 34 different species likely to be encountered in inshore waters.

Coarse Fishing for New Anglers by W. M. Hill. A practical introduction to the sport, written for beginners of all ages, this book has been designed to take the reader easily and interestingly through the progressive stages of his angling apprenticeship. First, he learns about rods, tackle, baits and the broad range of fish species and angling terms. Later, he gets down to action at the waterside in descriptive sequences showing how the earlier information on techniques is put into practice.